The Global Findex Database

2017

Measuring Financial Inclusion
and the Fintech Revolution

The Global Findex Database

2017

Measuring Financial Inclusion
and the Fintech Revolution

Asli Demirgüç-Kunt
Leora Klapper
Dorothe Singer
Saniya Ansar
Jake Hess

 **WORLD BANK GROUP**

CONTENTS

Figures

Maps

Table

FOREWORD

For those of us committed to advancing financial inclusion, no tool is of greater value than the Global Financial Inclusion (Global Findex) database. This invaluable data set provides a rigorous, multidimensional picture of where we stand and how far we have come in expanding access *for all* to the basic financial services people need to protect themselves against hardship and invest in their futures.

The Global Findex Database 2017: Measuring Financial Inclusion and the Fintech Revolution presents key findings from the Global Findex database, with detailed insight into how adults in more than 140 economies access accounts, make payments, save, borrow, and manage risk. As the data show, each economy has its own successes, challenges, and opportunities when it comes to financial inclusion. A growing body of research demonstrates the impact of country advances on significant priorities such as reducing poverty, hunger, and gender inequality. Today, member states at the United Nations are using Global Findex data to track progress toward the Sustainable Development Goals.

Dozens of national governments have adopted policies to expand financial inclusion. These and other global and national efforts are paying off. New Global Findex data reveal that globally the share of adults owning an account is now 69 percent, an increase of seven percentage points since 2014. These numbers translate into 515 million adults who have gained access to financial tools. The 2017 figures on overall account ownership continue the upward trajectory we've seen since the Global Findex database was first released—with financial inclusion rising 18 percentage points since 2011, when account ownership was 51 percent.

The 2017 Global Findex data reflect the continued evolution of financial inclusion. Recent progress has been driven by digital payments, government policies, and a new generation of financial services accessed through mobile phones and the internet.

The power of financial technology to expand access to and use of accounts is demonstrated most persuasively in Sub-Saharan Africa, where 21 percent of adults now have a mobile money account—nearly twice the share in 2014 and easily the highest of any region in the world. While mobile money has been centered in East Africa, the 2017 update reveals that it has spread to West Africa and beyond.

Digital technology is also transforming the payments landscape. Globally, 52 percent of adults have sent or received digital payments in the past year, up from 42 percent in 2014. Technology giants have moved into the financial sphere, leveraging deep customer knowledge to provide a broad range of financial services. Payments made through their technology platforms are facilitating higher account use in major emerging economies such as China, where 57 percent of account owners are using mobile phones or the internet to make purchases or pay bills—roughly twice the share in 2014.

Some advances have been made in helping women gain access to financial services. In India three years ago, men were 20 percentage points more likely than women to have an account. Today, India's gender gap has shrunk to 6 percentage points thanks to a strong government push to increase account ownership through biometric identification cards.

Still, in most of the world women continue to lag well behind men. Globally, 65 percent of women have an account compared with 72 percent of men, a gap of seven percentage points that is all but unchanged since 2011. Nor has equality in account ownership been achieved in other regards. The gap between rich and poor has not improved since 2014: account ownership is 13 percentage points higher among adults living in the wealthiest 60 percent of households within economies than among those in the poorest 40 percent. And urban populations continue to benefit from far broader access to finance than rural communities. In China around 200 million rural adults remain outside the formal financial system.

The continued involvement of businesses will be vital for unlocking opportunities to expand financial inclusion. Companies pay wages in cash to about 230 million unbanked adults worldwide; switching to electronic payrolls could help these workers join the formal financial system. Mobile phones and the internet also offer strong openings for progress: globally, one billion financially excluded adults already own a mobile phone and about 480 million have internet access.

But the private sector, governments, and development organizations all need to sharpen their focus on the use of accounts, which has stagnated for saving and borrowing. Without people actively using their accounts, the impact of our work will be lost.

The Global Findex database is an indispensable resource for those of us working to increase financial inclusion. I am proud to partner with the Global Findex team, and I thank the World Bank's Development Research Group and the Bill & Melinda Gates Foundation for supporting this crucial initiative. I hope governments, businesses, and development champions will continue to use *The Global Findex Database 2017: Measuring Financial Inclusion and the Fintech Revolution* and its trove of information as we redouble our efforts to deepen financial inclusion.

Her Majesty Queen Máxima of the Netherlands
UN Secretary-General's Special Advocate for Inclusive Finance for Development
Honorary Patron of the G-20's Global Partnership for Financial Inclusion

ACKNOWLEDGMENTS

The 2017 Global Findex database was prepared by the Finance and Private Sector Development Team of the Development Research Group, by a team led by Leora Klapper under the supervision of Asli Demirgüç-Kunt and comprising Saniya Ansar, Jake Hess, Deeksha Kokas, Adrienne Sigrid Larson, and Dorothe Singer. The work was carried out under the management of Shantayanan Devarajan. The team is grateful to Tito Cordella, Robert Cull, Loretta Michaels, Sebastian-A Molineus, Ceyla Pazarbasioglu-Dutz, Mahesh Uttamchandani, and World Bank colleagues in the Development Economics Vice Presidency and the Finance, Competitiveness & Innovation Global Practice as well as staff at the Bill & Melinda Gates Foundation, the Better Than Cash Alliance, the Consultative Group to Assist the Poor, the GSM Association, the G-20's Global Partnership for Financial Inclusion, and the Office of the UNSGSA (UN Secretary-General's Special Advocate for Inclusive Finance for Development) for providing substantive comments at different stages of the project. The team is also grateful for the excellent survey execution and related support provided by Gallup, Inc., under the direction of Jon Clifton and Joe Daly and with the support of Cynthia English and Neli Esipova.

The team is especially grateful to the Bill & Melinda Gates Foundation for providing financial support making the collection and dissemination of the data possible.

Maps were created by Tariq Afzal Khokhar and Andrew Michael Whitby from the World Bank's Development Data Group. Bruno Bonansea from the World Bank's Map Design Unit provided guidance on maps. A team at Communications Development Incorporated led by Bruce Ross-Larson managed the design and typesetting. Hank Isaac at 495 Digital designed the cover. Alison Strong provided editorial assistance. The production team included Patricia Katayama (acquisitions) and Susan Graham (project manager).

ABOUT THE GLOBAL FINDEX DATABASE

In 2011 the World Bank—with funding from the Bill & Melinda Gates Foundation—launched the Global Findex database, the world's most comprehensive data set on how adults save, borrow, make payments, and manage risk. Drawing on survey data collected in collaboration with Gallup, Inc., the Global Findex database covers more than 140 economies around the world. The initial survey round was followed by a second one in 2014 and by a third in 2017.

Compiled using nationally representative surveys of more than 150,000 adults age 15 and above in over 140 economies, the 2017 Global Findex database includes updated indicators on access to and use of formal and informal financial services. It has additional data on the use of financial technology (or fintech), including the use of mobile phones and the internet to conduct financial transactions. The data reveal opportunities to expand access to financial services among people who do not have an account—the unbanked—as well as to promote greater use of digital financial services among those who do have an account.

The Global Findex database has become a mainstay of global efforts to promote financial inclusion. In addition to being widely cited by scholars and development practitioners, Global Findex data are used to track progress toward the World Bank goal of Universal Financial Access by 2020 and the United Nations Sustainable Development Goals.

The database, the full text of the report, and the underlying country-level data for all figures—along with the questionnaire, the survey methodology, and other relevant materials—are available at http://www.worldbank.org/globalfindex.

All regional and global averages presented in this publication are population weighted. Regional averages include only developing economies (low- and middle-income economies as classified by the World Bank).

The reference citation for the 2017 Global Findex data is as follows:

Demirgüç-Kunt, Asli, Leora Klapper, Dorothe Singer, Saniya Ansar, and Jake Hess. 2018. *The Global Findex Database 2017: Measuring Financial Inclusion and the Fintech Revolution*. Washington, DC: World Bank.

OVERVIEW

Financial services can help drive development. They help people escape poverty by facilitating investments in their health, education, and businesses. And they make it easier to manage financial emergencies—such as a job loss or crop failure —that can push families into destitution.[1] Many poor people around the world lack the financial services that can serve these functions, such as bank accounts and digital payments. Instead, they rely on cash—which can be unsafe and hard to manage. That's why the World Bank has made it a key priority to promote financial inclusion—access to and use of formal financial services.

Why financial inclusion matters for development

A growing body of research reveals many potential development benefits from financial inclusion—especially from the use of digital financial services, including mobile money services, payment cards, and other financial technology (or fintech) applications. While the evidence is somewhat mixed, even studies that do not find positive results often point to possibilities for achieving better outcomes through careful attention to local needs.[2]

The benefits from financial inclusion can be wide ranging. For example, studies have shown that mobile money services—which allow users to store and transfer funds through a mobile phone—can help improve people's income-earning potential and thus reduce poverty. A study in Kenya found that access to mobile money services delivered big benefits, especially for women. It enabled women-headed households to increase their savings by more than a fifth; allowed 185,000 women to leave farming and develop business or retail activities; and helped reduce extreme poverty among women-headed households by 22 percent.[3]

Digital financial services can also help people manage financial risk—by making it easier for them to collect money from distant friends and relatives when times are tough. In Kenya researchers found that when hit with an unexpected drop in income, mobile money users did not reduce household spending—while nonusers and users with poor access to the mobile money network reduced their purchases of food and other items by 7–10 percent.[4]

In addition, digital financial services can lower the cost of receiving payments. In a five-month relief program in Niger, switching the monthly payment of government social benefits from cash to mobile phones saved the recipients 20 hours on average in overall travel and wait time to obtain the payments.[5]

Financial services can also help people accumulate savings and increase spending on necessities. After being provided with savings accounts, market vendors in Kenya, primarily women, saved at a higher rate and invested 60 percent more in their businesses.[6] Women-headed households in Nepal spent 15 percent more on nutritious foods (meat and fish) and 20 percent more on education after receiving free savings accounts.[7] And farmers in Malawi who had their earnings deposited into savings accounts spent 13 percent more on farming equipment and increased their crop values by 15 percent.[8]

For governments, switching from cash to digital payments can reduce corruption and improve efficiency. In India the leakage of funds for pension payments dropped by 47 percent (2.8 percentage points) when the payments were made through biometric smart cards rather than being handed out in cash.[9] In Niger, distributing social transfers through mobile phones rather than in cash reduced the variable cost of administering the benefits by 20 percent.[10]

Continued growth in account ownership

The Global Findex database shows that 515 million adults worldwide opened an account at a financial institution or through a mobile money provider between 2014 and 2017. This means that 69 percent of adults now have an account, up from 62 percent in 2014 and 51 percent in 2011. In high-income economies 94 percent of adults have an account; in developing economies 63 percent do. There is also wide variation in account ownership among individual economies (map O.1).

The vast majority of account owners have an account at a bank, a microfinance institution, or another type of regulated financial institution. Sub-Saharan Africa is the only region where the share of adults with a mobile money account exceeds 10 percent. This was also true in 2014. At that time East Africa was the region's mobile money hub. But mobile money accounts have since spread to new parts of Sub-Saharan Africa (map O.2). The share of adults with a mobile money account has now surpassed 30 percent in Côte d'Ivoire and Senegal—and 40 percent in Gabon.

Mobile money accounts have also taken root in economies outside Sub-Saharan Africa. In some, the share of adults with a mobile money account has reached about 20 percent or more—including Bangladesh, the Islamic Republic of Iran, Mongolia, and Paraguay.

Today, 69 percent of adults around the world have an account
Adults with an account (%), 2017

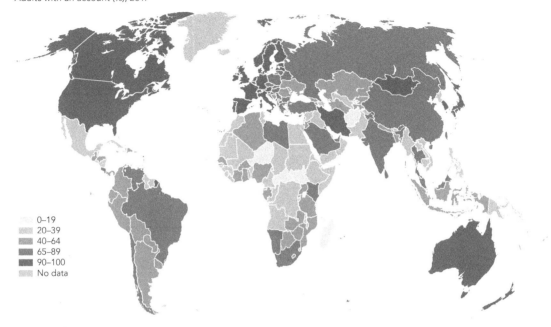

0–19
20–39
40–64
65–89
90–100
No data

Source: Global Findex database.

Mobile money accounts have spread more widely in Sub-Saharan Africa since 2014
Adults with a mobile money account (%)

2014   2017

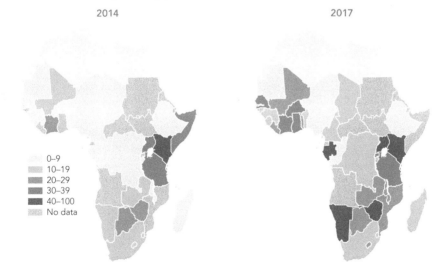

0–9
10–19
20–29
30–39
40–100
No data

Source: Global Findex database.
Note: Data are displayed only for economies in Sub-Saharan Africa.

The gender gap in account ownership persists in developing economies
Adults with an account (%)

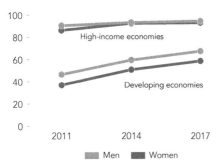

Source: Global Findex database.

Persistent inequality in account ownership

Even as account ownership continues to grow, inequalities persist. While 72 percent of men have an account, 65 percent of women do. That gender gap of 7 percentage points was also present in 2014 and 2011. In developing economies the gender gap remains unchanged at 9 percentage points (figure O.1).

Nor has the gap between richer and poorer narrowed. Among adults in the richest 60 percent of households within economies, 74 percent have an account. But among those in the poorest 40 percent, only 61 percent do, leaving a global gap of 13 percentage points. The difference is similar in developing economies, and neither gap has changed meaningfully since 2014. Account ownership is also lower among young adults, the less educated, and those who are out of the labor force.

But the picture is not entirely bleak. Consider India, where a strong government push to increase account ownership through biometric identification cards helped narrow both the gender gap and the gap between richer and poorer adults. And several developing economies have no significant gender gap, including Argentina, Indonesia, and South Africa.

Who remains unbanked—and reasons why

Globally, about 1.7 billion adults remain unbanked—without an account at a financial institution or through a mobile money provider. Because account ownership is nearly universal in high-income economies, virtually all these unbanked adults live in the developing world. Indeed, nearly half live in just seven developing economies: Bangladesh, China, India, Indonesia, Mexico, Nigeria, and Pakistan (map O.3).

Fifty-six percent of all unbanked adults are women. Women are overrepresented among the unbanked in economies where only a small share of adults are unbanked, such as China and India, as well as in those where half or more are, such as Bangladesh and Colombia.

Poorer people also account for a disproportionate share of the unbanked. Globally, half of unbanked adults come from the poorest 40 percent of households within their economy, the other half from the richest 60 percent. But the pattern varies among economies. In those where half or more of adults are unbanked, the unbanked are as likely to come from a poorer household as from a wealthier one. In economies where only about 20–30 percent of adults are unbanked, however, the unbanked are much more likely to be poor.

Globally, 1.7 billion adults lack an account
Adults without an account, 2017

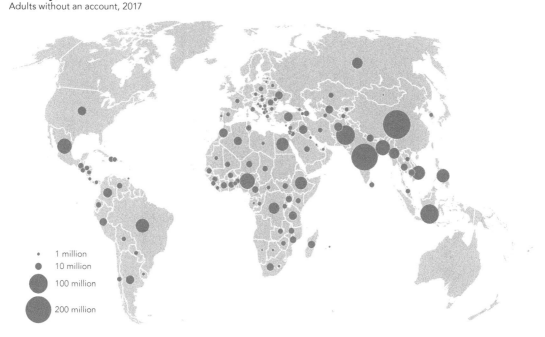

1 million
10 million
100 million
200 million

Source: Global Findex database.
Note: Data are not displayed for economies where the share of adults without an account is 5 percent or less.

Unbanked adults are more likely to have low educational attainment. In the developing world about half of all adults have a primary education or less. Among unbanked adults the share is close to two-thirds. Slightly more than a third of the unbanked have completed high school or postsecondary education.

Those active in the labor force are less likely to be unbanked. While about 37 percent of all adults in the developing world are out of the labor force, 47 percent of unbanked adults are. Among the unbanked, women are more likely than men to be out of the labor force.

To shed light on why people are unbanked, the 2017 Global Findex survey asked adults without a financial institution account why they do not have one. Most offered two reasons. The most common one was having too little money to use an account. Two-thirds cited this as a reason for not having a financial institution account, and roughly a fifth cited it as the sole reason. Cost and distance were each cited by about a quarter of those responding to the question, and a similar share said they do not have an account because a family member already has one. Lack of documentation and distrust in the financial system were both cited by roughly a fifth of adults without a financial institution account, and religious concerns by 6 percent.

How people make and receive payments

Most people make payments, such as for utility bills or to send money to relatives in another part of the country. And most receive payments, such as wages or government transfers. The 2017 Global Findex survey asked people what kinds of payments they make and receive and how they carry out these transactions—whether by using an account or in cash.

Payments from government

Globally, nearly a quarter of adults receive payments from the government—whether public sector wages, a public sector pension, or government transfers (social benefits such as subsidies, unemployment benefits, or payments for educational or medical expenses). In high-income economies 43 percent of adults receive such payments; the share is half as large in developing economies. Except in the poorest economies, most people getting government payments receive them into an account.

Payments for work

The Global Findex data also cover payments for private sector wages as well as other payments for work—such as payments for the sale of agricultural products. Globally, 28 percent of adults receive private sector wages—46 percent of adults in high-income economies and 24 percent in developing ones. In high-income economies most receive these payments into an account; in developing economies only about half do so.

About 15 percent of adults in developing economies receive payments for the sale of agricultural products—and almost all receive these payments in cash. But in some economies in Sub-Saharan Africa—such as Ghana, Kenya, and Zambia—about 40 percent of those getting agricultural payments receive them into an account, in most cases a mobile money account.

Domestic remittance payments

Domestic remittances—money sent to or received from relatives or friends in another part of the country—are an important part of the economy in many places. This is particularly so in Sub-Saharan Africa, where nearly half of adults send or receive such payments. In developing economies those sending or receiving domestic remittances are most likely to use an account to do so: 46 percent rely on an account, while 27 percent use cash, 19 percent an over-the-counter service, and 8 percent some other method. This pattern generally holds among many developing economies, including those in Sub-Saharan Africa.

How people access and use their accounts

Owning an account is an important first step toward financial inclusion. But to fully benefit from having an account, people need to be able to use it in safe and convenient ways. The Global Findex database provides insights into not only who owns an account but whether and how people use their account for payments.

For digital payments

Globally, 52 percent of adults—or 76 percent of account owners—reported having made or received at least one digital payment using their account in the past year. In high-income economies the share was 91 percent of adults (97 percent of account owners), in developing economies 44 percent of adults (70 percent of account owners).

The use of digital payments is on the rise. The share of adults around the world making or receiving digital payments increased by 11 percentage points between 2014 and 2017 (figure O.2). In developing economies the share of adults using digital payments rose by 12 percentage points, to 44 percent.

FIGURE O.2

More people who have an account are using it for digital payments
Adults with an account (%)

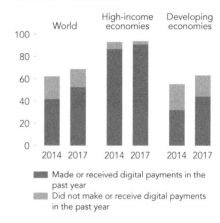

Source: Global Findex database.

Through a mobile phone or the internet

Mobile phones and the internet increasingly offer an alternative to debit and credit cards for making direct payments from an account. In high-income economies 51 percent of adults (55 percent of account owners) reported making at least one financial transaction in the past year using a mobile phone or the internet. In developing economies 19 percent of adults (30 percent of account owners) reported making at least one direct payment using a mobile money account, a mobile phone, or the internet.

Ways of using a mobile phone
When it comes to using a mobile phone for financial services, China and Kenya represent two different models. In China mobile financial services are provided primarily through third-party payment service providers such as Alipay and WeChat using smartphone apps linked to an account at a bank or another type of financial institution. By contrast, in Kenya mobile financial services are offered mainly by mobile network operators, and mobile money accounts do not need to be linked to an account at a financial institution.

In Kenya most account owners have both a financial institution account and a mobile money account. This is reflected in how people make mobile payments. Forty percent of adults use only a mobile money account to make such payments.

Another 29 percent rely on two methods—using a mobile money account and using a mobile phone or the internet to access their financial institution account. And 2 percent make mobile payments only by using a mobile phone or the internet to access their financial institution account. In China 40 percent of adults make mobile payments.

Ways of using the internet

Another way that people make digital payments is by using the internet, to pay bills or to buy something online. Globally, 29 percent of adults used the internet for one of these two purposes in the past year. But the share ranged from 68 percent of adults in high-income economies to 49 percent in China to an average of just 11 percent in developing economies excluding China.

Buying something online does not necessarily mean paying for it online. In many developing economies people commonly pay cash on delivery for internet orders. To measure how common that practice is, the 2017 Global Findex survey asked people in developing economies how they pay for internet purchases. On average in all developing economies except China, 53 percent of adults who made an internet purchase in the past 12 months paid for it in cash on delivery. In China, by contrast, 85 percent of adults who bought something online also paid for it online.

Inactive accounts

Not all people who have an account actively use it. Globally, about a fifth of account owners reported making no deposit and no withdrawal—in digital form or otherwise—in the past 12 months and therefore have what can be considered an inactive account.[11] The share with an inactive account varies across economies but is especially high for many economies in South Asia.

Patterns in saving, credit, and financial resilience

Saving money, accessing credit, and managing financial risk are all key aspects of financial inclusion. Global Findex data show how and why people save and borrow and shed light on their ability to meet unexpected expenses.

Saving for the future

About half of adults worldwide reported saving money in the past year. In high-income economies 71 percent reported saving, while in developing economies 43 percent did (figure O.3). People save money in different ways. Many save formally, such as by using an account at a financial institution. In high-income economies more than three-quarters of savers (55 percent of all adults) save using this method; in developing economies just under half of savers (21 percent of all adults) save this way. A common alternative is to save semiformally, by using a savings club—particularly common in Sub-Saharan Africa—or by entrusting savings to someone outside the family. And some save in some other way. This may include simply saving in cash at home ("under the mattress") or saving in the form of livestock, jewelry, or real estate. It may also include using investment products offered by equity and other traded markets or purchasing government securities.

Savings patterns also vary by gender and income. In developing economies men are 6 percentage points more likely than women to save at a financial institution, while wealthier adults are 15 percentage points more likely than poorer adults to do so. In high-income economies wealthier adults are 23 percentage points more likely than poorer adults to save formally.

Nearly half of adults in high-income economies reported saving for old age. In developing economies only 16 percent did. And in high-income and developing economies alike, 14 percent reported saving to start, operate, or expand a business. Saving for a business is more common in many Sub-Saharan African economies—reported by 29 percent or more of adults in Ethiopia, Kenya, and Nigeria, for example.

Borrowing money

About half of adults worldwide reported borrowing money in the past year. A higher share did so in high-income economies, where most borrowers rely on formal credit, extended by a financial institution or through a credit card. By contrast, borrowers in developing economies are most likely to turn to family or friends (figure O.4).

For what purposes do people borrow? One common purpose is to buy land or a home, the largest financial investment that many people make in their life. In 2017, 27 percent of adults in high-income economies reported having an outstanding housing loan from a bank or another type of financial institution. In contrast, that share was typically less than 10 percent in developing economies.

Coming up with emergency funds

To measure financial resilience, the 2017 Global Findex survey asked respondents whether it would

FIGURE O.3

Globally, more than half of adults who save choose to do so at a financial institution
Adults saving any money in the past year (%), 2017

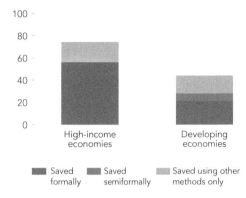

Source: Global Findex database.
Note: People may save in multiple ways, but categories are constructed to be mutually exclusive. *Saved formally* includes all adults who saved any money formally. *Saved semiformally* includes all adults who saved any money semiformally but not formally. Data on semiformal saving are not collected in most high-income economies.

FIGURE O.4

Borrowers are more likely to rely on formal credit in high-income economies than in developing ones
Adults borrowing any money in the past year (%), 2017

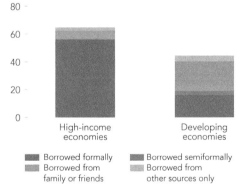

Source: Global Findex database.
Note: People may borrow from multiple sources, but categories are constructed to be mutually exclusive. *Borrowed formally* includes all adults who borrowed any money from a financial institution or through the use of a credit card. *Borrowed semiformally* includes all adults who borrowed any money semiformally (from a savings club) but not formally. *Borrowed from family or friends* excludes adults who borrowed formally or semiformally.

People in high-income economies are more likely to be able to raise emergency funds—and to do so through savings

Adults able to raise emergency funds (%), 2017

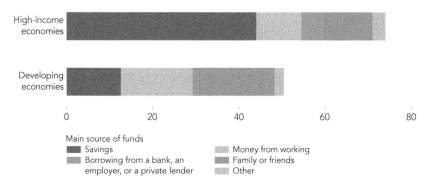

Source: Global Findex database.
Note: Other includes all respondents who chose "selling assets," "other sources," "don't know," or "refuse" as their response for main source of emergency funds.

be possible to come up with an amount equal to 1/20 of gross national income (GNI) per capita in local currency within the next month. It also asked what their main source of funding would be. Those in high-income economies were far more likely to say they could raise emergency funds (figure O.5). Among the respondents saying they could come up with funds, most in high-income economies said they would rely on savings, while most in developing economies said they would turn to family or friends or use money from working. Among those in developing economies who cited savings as their main source of funding, 85 percent have an account, but only 50 percent reported having saved at a financial institution.

Increasing financial inclusion through digital technology

Since being launched in 2011, the Global Findex database has provided insights into ways to increase financial inclusion. The 2017 edition, for the first time, features data on mobile phone ownership and access to the internet, revealing unprecedented opportunities to reduce the number of adults without an account and to help those who have one use it more often.

Of course, digital technology alone is not enough to increase financial inclusion. To ensure that people benefit from digital financial services requires a well-developed payments system, good physical infrastructure, appropriate regulations, and vigorous consumer protection safeguards. And whether digital or analogue, financial services need to be tailored to the needs of disadvantaged groups such as women, poor people, and first-time users of financial services, who may have low literacy and numeracy skills.

Having a simple mobile phone can potentially open access to mobile money accounts and other financial services. Having access to the internet as well

Two-thirds of unbanked adults have a mobile phone
Adults without an account owning a mobile phone, 2017

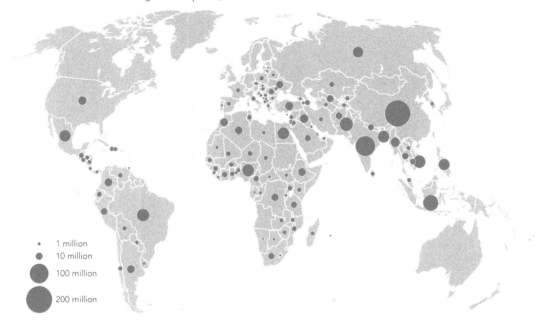

Sources: Global Findex database; Gallup World Poll 2017.
Note: Data are not displayed for economies where the share of adults without an account is 5 percent or less.

expands the range of possibilities. These technologies could help overcome barriers that unbanked adults say prevent them from accessing financial services.
Mobile phones could eliminate the need to travel long distances to a financial
institution. And by lowering the cost of providing financial services, digital technology might increase their affordability.

How many unbanked adults have a mobile phone? Globally, about 1.1 billion—or
about two-thirds of all unbanked adults. In India and Mexico more than 50 percent of the unbanked have a mobile phone; in China 82 percent do (map O.4).

Fewer unbanked adults have both a mobile phone and access to the internet in
some form—whether through a smartphone, a home computer, an internet café,
or some other way. Globally, the share is about a quarter. But just as for accounts,
access to digital technology—whether a mobile phone or both a mobile phone
and the internet—tends to be lower among women, poorer adults, the less educated, and other traditionally disadvantaged groups.

Ways to increase the ownership of accounts

By moving routine cash payments into accounts, governments and businesses
could help dramatically reduce the number of unbanked adults. Governments
make several types of payments to people—paying wages to public sector

About 235 million unbanked adults receive agricultural payments in cash
Adults without an account receiving payments for agricultural products in the past year in cash only, 2017

1 million
10 million
100 million

Source: Global Findex database.
Note: Data are not displayed for economies where the share of adults without an account is 5 percent or less or the share receiving payments for agricultural products is 10 percent or less.

workers, distributing public sector pensions, and providing government transfers to those needing social benefits. Digitizing these payments could reduce the number of unbanked adults by up to 100 million globally. Many of these adults have the basic technology needed to receive these payments in digital form. Of the 60 million unbanked adults worldwide who receive government transfers in cash, two-thirds have a mobile phone.

Even bigger opportunities are available in the private sector. Globally, about 230 million unbanked adults work in the private sector and get paid in cash only —and 78 percent of these wage earners have a mobile phone.

Unbanked farmers could benefit from the security and convenience of digital payments for agricultural sales. About 235 million unbanked adults worldwide receive cash payments for the sale of agricultural products (map O.5)—and 59 percent of them have a mobile phone. Digitizing agribusiness supply chains could also build payment histories and help expand access to credit and insurance for small farmers.

Ways to increase the use of accounts

While financial inclusion starts with having an account, the benefits come from actively using that account—for saving money, for managing risk, for making or

A billion adults who have an account still pay utility bills in cash
Adults with an account paying utility bills in the past year in cash only, 2017

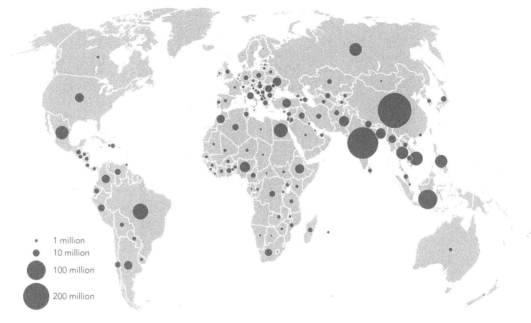

- 1 million
- 10 million
- 100 million
- 200 million

Source: Global Findex database.

receiving payments. Global Findex data point to many opportunities to help people who already have an account make better use of it.

Globally, a billion adults who have an account still use cash to pay utility bills (map O.6). If more utility providers offered an attractive option for paying bills digitally, both sides could benefit from greater efficiency.

Many adults who are employed and have an account still get paid in cash. About 300 million account owners worldwide work in the private sector and get paid in cash, while roughly 275 million account owners receive cash payments for the sale of agricultural products.

And roughly 280 million account owners in developing economies use cash or an over-the-counter service to send or receive domestic remittances—including 10 million in Bangladesh and 65 million in India.

Notes

1. For overviews of how financial inclusion can drive development, see Karlan and others (2016); and Demirgüç-Kunt, Klapper, and Singer (2017).
2. A study on extending basic, no-frills accounts to the rural poor in Chile, Malawi, and Uganda, for example, found no evidence that doing so led to overall increases in savings

or improvements in such outcomes as health, schooling, or consumption (Dupas and others, forthcoming). The study speculates that several factors limited the impact of expanding access to accounts: the accounts not being tailored to specific needs, high transaction costs in using the accounts, and the individuals included in the study being poorer compared with those in other studies. Moreover, innovations making it easier and less costly to carry out financial transactions can have unintended consequences. In Kenya, for example, a study providing account owners with free automated teller machine (ATM) cards increased the accessibility of accounts, but this made accounts less attractive to women who used them to keep personal savings away from husbands with greater bargaining power (Schaner 2017).

3. Suri and Jack (2016).
4. Jack and Suri (2014).
5. Aker and others (2016).
6. Dupas and Robinson (2013). However, the study found no such impact for men working as bicycle taxi drivers.
7. Prina (2015).
8. Brune and others (2016).
9. Muralidharan, Niehaus, and Sukhtankar (2016).
10. Aker and others (2016).
11. It is not possible to ascertain whether accounts with no deposit and no withdrawal in the past 12 months are "dormant," as they may be used for long-term saving.

1 ACCOUNT OWNERSHIP

Globally, 69 percent of adults have an account. That gives them an important financial tool. Accounts provide a safe way to store money and build savings for the future. They also make it easier to pay bills, access credit, make purchases, and send or receive remittances. Having an account is therefore used by the World Bank and others as a marker of financial inclusion.

The 2017 Global Findex database defines account ownership as having an individual or jointly owned account either at a financial institution or through a mobile money provider. The first category includes accounts at a bank or another type of formal, regulated financial institution, such as a credit union, a cooperative, or a microfinance institution.[1] The second consists of mobile phone–based services, not linked to a financial institution, that are used to pay bills or to send

MAP 1.1

Account ownership varies widely around the world
Adults with an account (%), 2017

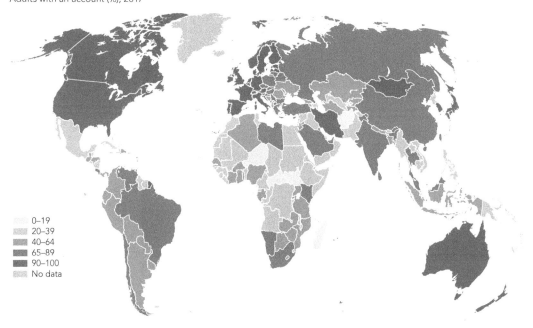

0–19
20–39
40–64
65–89
90–100
No data

Source: Global Findex database.

or receive money. These mobile money accounts allow people to store money and to send and receive electronic payments.[2]

To identify people with a mobile money account, the 2017 Global Findex survey asked respondents about their use of specific services available in their economy —such as M-PESA, MTN Mobile Money, Airtel Money, or Orange Money—and included in the GSM Association's Mobile Money for the Unbanked (GSMA MMU) database. The definition of a mobile money account is limited to services that can be used without an account at a financial institution. People using a mobile money account linked to their financial institution are considered to have an account at a financial institution. The question on mobile money accounts was asked only in the 77 economies—among the 144 included in the survey—where the GSMA MMU database indicates that mobile money accounts were available at the time the survey was carried out.

Account ownership around the world

Account ownership is nearly universal in high-income economies, where 94 percent of adults have an account. In developing economies—those classified by the World Bank as low or middle income—the share is 63 percent.

But there is wide variation in account ownership among economies (map 1.1). Indeed, there are large differences even within income groups (figure 1.1). Consider the lower-middle-income group, where the share of adults with an account varies from about 20 percent in Cambodia, Mauritania, and Pakistan to as high as 93 percent in Mongolia. Among high-income economies the share with an account ranges from 64 percent in Uruguay to 100 percent in such economies as Australia, Denmark, and the Netherlands.

Among the 69 percent of adults around the world who are account owners, the vast majority have an account at a financial institution: 64 percent of all adults

FIGURE 1.1
Account ownership differs substantially even within income groups
Adults with an account (%), 2017

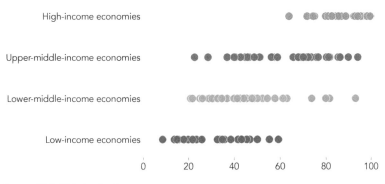

Source: Global Findex database.

reported having a financial institution account only; 3 percent having a financial institution account as well as a mobile money account; and 1 percent a mobile money account only.

What are the trends since 2011?

The first Global Findex survey was completed in 2011, followed by a second round in 2014 and the latest one in 2017. Globally over those intervals, the share of adults with an account rose from 51 percent to 62 percent and then to 69 percent (figure 1.2).

Among developing economies, however, the growth in account ownership has been far from uniform (figure 1.3). In India the share of adults with an account has more than doubled since 2011, to 80 percent. An important factor driving this increase was a government policy launched in 2014 to boost account ownership among unbanked adults through biometric identification cards.[3] This policy benefited traditionally excluded groups and helped ensure inclusive growth in account ownership. Between 2014 and 2017 account ownership in India rose by more than 30 percentage points among women as well as among adults in the poorest 40 percent of households. Among men and among adults in the wealthiest 60 percent of households it increased by about 20 percentage points. Indonesia also saw equitable growth in account ownership among men and women as the overall share of adults with an account rose from 20 percent in 2011 to 49 percent in 2017.

Some economies have had gains in account ownership but missed out on opportunities for greater progress because women were insufficiently included. In Pakistan, for example, account ownership has doubled since 2011, though it started from a low base of 10 percent. But while it surged among men, it stagnated among women. In Ethiopia account ownership has risen by 18 percentage points among men since 2014, roughly twice the size of the increase among women. Bangladesh has also had uneven progress, with slower gains among

FIGURE 1.2

Financial institution accounts have fueled the growth in account ownership since 2011

Adults with an account (%)

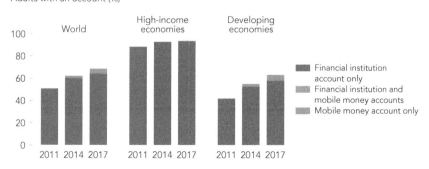

Source: Global Findex database.
Note: No data are available for the share of adults with a mobile money account for 2011.

FIGURE 1.3

Account ownership has grown in some developing economies, stagnated in others

Adults with an account (%)

Legend: 2011 2014 2017

Source: Global Findex database.
Note: No data are available for Ethiopia for 2011.

women. Yet the picture is not entirely bleak in these economies. Most have seen account ownership rise among women and poorer adults. But more inclusive growth in account ownership would have led to faster overall progress.

Account ownership has remained largely unchanged in developing economies where it was already about 70 percent or more in 2014, such as Brazil, China, Malaysia, and South Africa.

How important are mobile money accounts?

The Global Findex survey first collected data on mobile money accounts in 2014. These data showed that 12 percent of adults in Sub-Saharan Africa had a mobile money account, while 2 percent did globally. Today Sub-Saharan Africa remains the global leader in the use of mobile money: 21 percent of adults in the region have a mobile money account. Among this group, nearly half reported having only a mobile money account, while the other half reported having a financial institution account as well.

Mobile money accounts are particularly widespread in Kenya, where 73 percent of adults have one, as well as in Uganda and Zimbabwe, where about 50 percent do (map 1.2). Sub-Saharan Africa is also home to all 10 economies worldwide where more adults have a mobile money account than have a financial institution account: Burkina Faso, Chad, Côte d'Ivoire, Gabon, Kenya, Mali, Senegal, Tanzania, Uganda, and Zimbabwe.

In 2014 mobile money accounts were concentrated largely in East Africa. Now these accounts have spread to West Africa and beyond. In West Africa the share of adults owning a mobile money account has risen to about 33 percent in Burkina Faso, Côte d'Ivoire, and Senegal—and to 39 percent in Ghana. And it has reached nearly 45 percent in both Gabon and Namibia.

MAP 1.2
Mobile money accounts have spread more widely in Sub-Saharan Africa since 2014
Adults with a mobile money account (%)

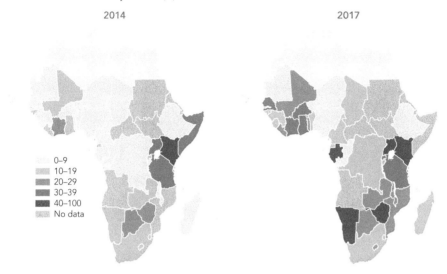

Source: Global Findex database.
Note: Data are displayed only for economies in Sub-Saharan Africa.

Sub-Saharan Africa may be the only region where more than 10 percent of adults have a mobile money account, but the technology has taken root in other parts of the world as well. In Haiti the share of adults with a mobile money account rose from 4 percent in 2014 to 14 percent in 2017. In Bangladesh the share jumped from 3 percent to 21 percent. Other economies too have seen an increase from the low single digits to about 20 percent or more—including Chile, the Islamic Republic of Iran, and Mongolia. Three years ago in Turkey, few adults had a mobile money account. Now 16 percent do. In Paraguay 29 percent have a mobile money account.

But these economies are not typical of global trends. Outside Sub-Saharan Africa mobile money accounts did not drive the growth in overall account ownership between 2011 and 2017. Most new accounts opened in this period were financial institution accounts (see figure 1.2).

Within Sub-Saharan Africa the share of adults with a financial institution account has risen by a modest 4 percentage points since 2014, while the share with a mobile money account has grown roughly twice as fast—increasing by 9 percentage points. But the extent to which mobile money accounts raised overall account ownership between 2014 and 2017 varies among economies in the region. In Côte d'Ivoire the share of adults with only a mobile money account increased by 8 percentage points, while the share with both types of accounts or only a financial institution account stagnated. Trends were largely

FIGURE 1.4

Mobile money has boosted account ownership in parts of Sub-Saharan Africa
Adults with an account (%)

FIGURE 1.5

Mobile money can play an important part in fragile and conflict-affected economies
Adults with an account (%), 2017

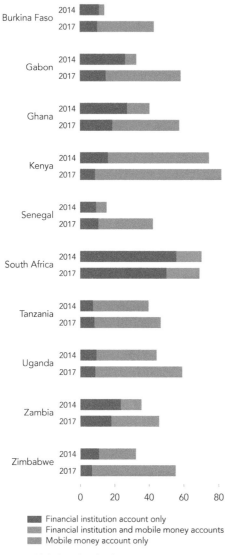

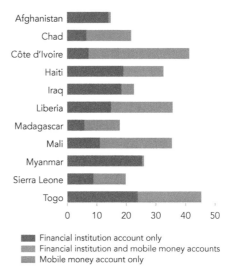

Financial institution account only
Financial institution and mobile money accounts
Mobile money account only

Source: Global Findex database.
Note: The figure shows only fragile and conflict-affected economies for which data on mobile money accounts are collected.

similar in Tanzania and Uganda (figure 1.4). In some economies—such as Burkina Faso, Gabon, Ghana, and Senegal—there were large increases in the share of adults with only a mobile money account as well as in the share with both types of accounts. And in still others—such as Kenya, Zambia, and Zimbabwe—the biggest growth occurred in the share with both types of accounts.

Financial institution account only
Financial institution and mobile money accounts
Mobile money account only

Source: Global Findex database.

Mobile money accounts play an important part in some fragile and conflict-affected economies, including areas requiring urgent emergency responses, such as Ebola-affected West Africa and earthquake-stricken Haiti. Overall account ownership is low in these economies, with only 27 percent of adults reporting having an account, but mobile money accounts provide an important boost in some of them. In Haiti as well as fragile and conflict-affected economies in Sub-Saharan Africa more than 40 percent of account owners have a mobile money account (figure 1.5). And in Côte d'Ivoire 83 percent of account owners have a mobile money account, 64 percent a mobile money account only.

Gender gaps in account ownership

The growth in account ownership since 2011 has not benefited all groups equally. Women still are less likely than men to have an account. Globally, 72 percent of men and 65 percent of women have an account, a gender gap of 7 percentage points (figure 1.6). The gender gap is similar in developing economies, with 67 percent of men but only 59 percent of women having an account.

Indeed, most developing economies have a gender gap in account ownership, though the size varies. In Bangladesh, Pakistan, and Turkey, for example, the gender gap is nearly 30 percentage points (figure 1.7). Other developing economies with a double-digit gender gap include Morocco, Mozambique, Peru, Rwanda, and Zambia. Smaller gaps are found in such economies as Brazil and India.

Some developing economies have no appreciable gender gap. Several of these are in East Asia and the Pacific, such as Cambodia and Myanmar—or in Europe and Central Asia, including Azerbaijan, Belarus, the Kyrgyz Republic, the Russian Federation, and Serbia (figure 1.8). Other developing economies with no significant gender gap include Bolivia, Namibia, South Africa, Sri Lanka, and Vietnam. And in a few developing economies—such as Argentina, Indonesia, and the Philippines—women are more likely than men to have an account.

The size of the gender gap in account ownership varies across economies
Adults with an account (%), 2017

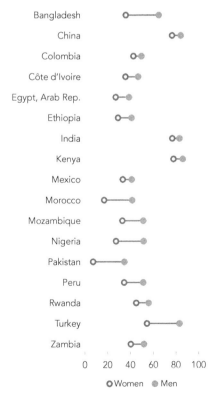

Source: Global Findex database.

Overall in developing economies, women are less likely than men to have an account
Adults with an account (%), 2017

Source: Global Findex database.

FIGURE 1.8
Some developing economies have no appreciable gender gap in account ownership—and a few have one that goes the other way
Adults with an account (%), 2017

O Women ● Men

Source: Global Findex database.

There is no discernible gender gap on average in high-income economies. But some economies in this group do have one. In Chile and Uruguay, for example, the share of men with an account is 6–7 percentage points higher than the share of women with one, while in Saudi Arabia the gender gap is 22 percentage points. In the United Arab Emirates account ownership is nearly universal among men, at 93 percent, while among women the share with an account drops to 76 percent.

How have gender gaps changed since 2011?

Gender gaps in account ownership remain mostly stuck where they were in 2011 and 2014. At 7 percentage points, the global gender gap is virtually the same today as it was in 2011 and 2014 (figure 1.9). The average gender gap in developing economies is also unchanged. None of the three rounds of the Global Findex survey found evidence of a significant gender gap in high-income economies on average.

At the economy level too, gender gaps have mostly remained stable. Economies that had no gender gap in 2014 generally still do not have one; the converse is also true. But there are exceptions. In 2014 no gender gap was found in Burkina Faso or Ethiopia. Since then these two

FIGURE 1.9
Gender gaps in account ownership have persisted over time
Adults with an account (%)

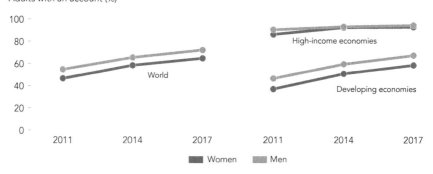

■ Women ■ Men

Source: Global Findex database.

economies have seen big growth in account ownership—but more among men than among women. As a result, both now have a double-digit gender gap in account ownership.

In some economies a large gender gap is slowing national progress in financial inclusion. Take Algeria, where 56 percent of men have an account but only 29 percent of women do, pulling the overall rate of account ownership down to 43 percent (figure 1.10). The rates are similar in such economies as Burkina Faso, Jordan, Mozambique, Nigeria, and Peru. Any effort to increase overall account ownership in these economies needs to prioritize financial inclusion for women.

Other economies have moved in the opposite direction. In India in 2014 men were 20 percentage points more likely than women to have an account. That gap has shrunk to 6 percentage points. Bolivia's gender gap, at 8 percentage points in 2014, has disappeared as account ownership has surpassed 50 percent among both men and women.

Is mobile money helping women get equal access to accounts?

The spread of mobile money accounts has created new opportunities to better serve women, poor people, and other groups traditionally excluded from the formal financial system. Indeed, there are some early signs that mobile money accounts might be helping to close the gender gap.

FIGURE 1.10

Large gender gaps in account ownership are holding back overall progress in financial inclusion in some economies
Adults with an account (%), 2017

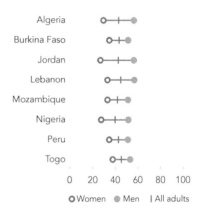

Source: Global Findex database.

Consider the eight economies where 20 percent or more of adults have a mobile money account only: Burkina Faso, Côte d'Ivoire, Gabon, Kenya, Senegal, Tanzania, Uganda, and Zimbabwe. These economies all have a statistically significant gap between men and women in the overall share with an account as well as in the share with both a financial institution account and a mobile money account.

But just two of them—Burkina Faso and Tanzania—have a gender gap in the share owning a mobile money account only (figure 1.11). The other six have no such gender gap. In Côte d'Ivoire, for example, men are twice as likely as women to have a financial institution account—yet women are just as likely as men to have a mobile money account only. In Kenya men are 18 percentage points more likely to have a financial institution account; they are also 18 percentage points more likely to have both types of accounts. But women are 11 percentage points more likely than men to have a mobile money account only.

FIGURE 1.11

In some economies mobile money accounts might be helping to narrow the gender gap in financial inclusion
Adults with an account (%), 2017

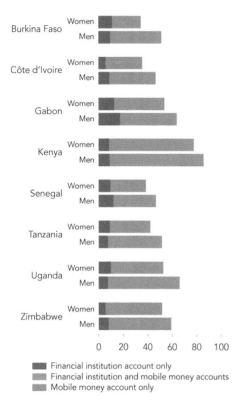

Legend:
- Financial institution account only
- Financial institution and mobile money accounts
- Mobile money account only

Source: Global Findex database.
Note: The figure shows only the economies where 20 percent or more of adults have a mobile money account only.

These results are encouraging, though it is still too early to say whether and how mobile money accounts can close the gender gap. Many more years of data collection and research are needed to truly understand any connections between mobile money accounts and gender inequality in account ownership and use of formal financial services. Meanwhile, the distinctions between types of accounts may begin to blur as more financial institutions design services tailored to the needs of poor people and as more mobile money operators enter into partnerships with financial institutions.

Gaps in account ownership between richer and poorer

On average around the world, poorer adults are less likely than wealthier ones to have an account. Among adults in the richest 60 percent of households within economies, 74 percent have an account. Among those in the poorest 40 percent of households, 61 percent do. That leaves a global gap between these two groups of 13 percentage points (figure 1.12). The average gap across developing economies is similar and accounts for much of the global gap. In high-income economies account ownership is nearly universal among both groups.

In most developing economies the gap in account ownership between richer and poorer adults reaches double digits. This is often true even in those where the overall share of adults with an account is relatively high, at about 70 percent or more. In Brazil and China, for example, account ownership is about 20 percentage points higher among wealthier adults than among poorer ones (figure 1.13). But sizable gaps also exist in economies where overall account ownership is relatively low, at about 50 percent or less. In the Arab Republic of Egypt, Ethiopia, Indonesia, Mexico, Nigeria, and Vietnam the gap is roughly 20 percentage points. Put differently, in these economies wealthier adults are about twice as likely as poorer ones to have an account.

FIGURE 1.12

Poorer adults are less likely than wealthier ones to have an account

Adults with an account (%), 2017

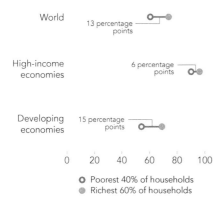

Source: Global Findex database.
Note: Data for the poorest 40 percent and richest 60 percent of households are based on household income quintiles within economies.

FIGURE 1.13

Developing economies tend to have a large gap in account ownership between richer and poorer adults

Adults with an account (%), 2017

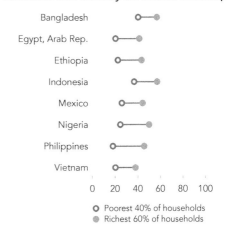

Source: Global Findex database.

On average, high-income economies do not have a large gap in account ownership between richer and poorer adults. But a few do have one —including Chile, the Czech Republic, Hungary, Israel, the Slovak Republic, and Uruguay, all of which have a double-digit gap between adults in the richest 60 percent of households and those in the poorest 40 percent.

Another way to assess such gaps is to compare account ownership among the very poorest with that among the very richest. In the United States account ownership is limited to only 79 percent of adults in the poorest 20 percent of households, while it is nearly universal among those in the richest 20 percent. By contrast, five of the country's fellow members of the Group of Seven (G-7)—Canada, France, Germany, Japan, and the United Kingdom—have no rich-poor gap in account ownership, while the sixth, Italy, has a smaller one of 13 percentage points.

How have gaps between richer and poorer changed since 2011?

The global gap in account ownership between richer and poorer has changed little since the initial Global Findex data were collected. In 2011 wealthier adults were 17 percentage points more likely than poorer ones to have an account, and

ACCOUNT OWNERSHIP | **27**

FIGURE 1.14

The gaps in account ownership between richer and poorer have changed little since 2011

Adults with an account (%)

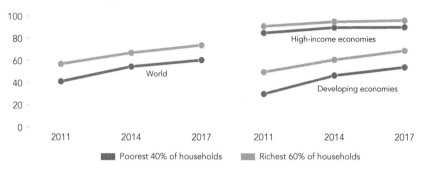

Source: Global Findex database.
Note: Data for the poorest 40 percent and richest 60 percent of households are based on household income quintiles within economies.

this gap is much the same now (figure 1.14). In developing economies on average, the gap narrowed slightly between 2011 and 2014, from 20 percentage points to 14 percentage points, and has not changed significantly since then.

In most individual economies too, the gaps have remained largely unchanged since 2011. But in some economies government policies have helped boost account ownership among poorer adults. One of these is India. In 2014 adults in the richest 60 percent of its households were 15 percentage points more likely than those in the poorest 40 percent to have an account. Since then, thanks in part to a government policy aimed at increasing financial inclusion, account ownership has risen among wealthier and poorer adults alike—narrowing the gap to 5 percentage points. In Thailand, because account ownership grew among poorer adults while stagnating among wealthier ones, the gap shrank by almost half between 2014 and 2017, from 12 percentage points to 7 percentage points. But in Turkey during the same period, because account ownership increased sharply among wealthier adults but only modestly among poorer ones, the gap grew from 8 percentage points to 20 percentage points.

Are mobile money accounts helping to shrink the gaps?

There are hints that mobile money accounts may be helping to reduce the gaps between richer and poorer in account ownership. Consider again the eight economies where 20 percent or more of adults have a mobile money account only. All of them have a statistically significant gap between richer and poorer adults in the share owning both a financial institution account and a mobile money account. But only half of them—Burkina Faso, Côte d'Ivoire, Senegal, and Uganda —have such a gap in the share owning a mobile money account only (figure 1.15). And in two of them, Kenya and Zimbabwe, poorer adults are more likely than wealthier ones to have a mobile money account only.

This suggests that mobile money accounts might be helping to increase access to financial services for poorer adults—and thus reducing inequality between rich and poor in financial inclusion. But a better understanding of this relationship will require more data and research.

Differences in account ownership by other individual characteristics

Gender and income are not the only individual characteristics that appear to matter for the likelihood of owning an account. Grouping people by age, education level, employment status, or rural residence can also reveal important differences in account ownership.

What are the differences by age group?

Account ownership is higher among older adults than among young adults. Globally, 72 percent of adults age 25 and older have an account, while only 56 percent of those ages 15–24 do (figure 1.16). The pattern is on average similar in both high-income and developing economies.

The size of the gap between the two age groups varies among developing economies. In Brazil account ownership is 30 percentage points higher among older adults than among young ones (figure 1.17). In Turkey the gap between the age groups is similar to the global average. Yet in Indonesia and Vietnam there is no major difference in account ownership between the age groups, and in China young adults are 8 percentage points more likely than older ones to have an account.

FIGURE 1.15

Mobile money accounts might be helping to reduce the gap in financial inclusion between richer and poorer in some economies
Adults with an account (%), 2017

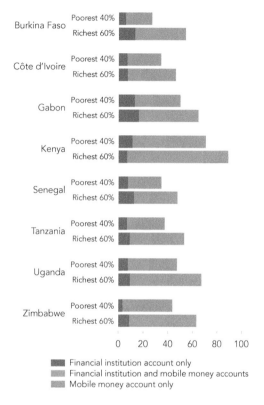

Source: Global Findex database.
Note: The figure shows only the economies where 20 percent or more of adults have a mobile money account only. *Poorest 40%* and *richest 60%* refer to households, grouped by income quintiles.

The story for mobile money accounts is different in some economies, with young adults more likely than older adults to have one. In Chile young adults are 5 percentage points more likely than older adults to have a mobile money account; the gap is roughly twice as large in Bangladesh and the Islamic Republic of Iran. But in Mongolia and Paraguay older adults are more likely than young adults to have a mobile money account. And in still other economies there is no significant difference in mobile money account ownership between the two age groups—including Burkina Faso, Kenya, Tanzania, Uganda, and Zambia.

FIGURE 1.16
Older adults are more likely than young adults to have an account
Adults with an account (%), 2017

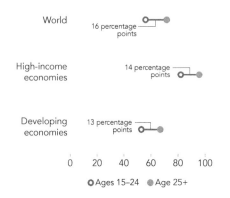

Source: Global Findex database.
Note: The global gap between the age groups is larger than the average gap for high-income and developing economies because in high-income economies adults are relatively more likely to have an account and to belong to the older age group while in developing economies adults are relatively more likely to not have an account and to belong to the younger age group.

FIGURE 1.17
The gap in account ownership between older adults and young adults varies widely among developing economies
Adults with an account (%), 2017

Source: Global Findex database.

What are the patterns by education level?

Account ownership is lower among less educated adults. Globally, 56 percent of adults with a primary education or less have an account, compared with 76 percent of those who have completed secondary school and 92 percent of those with higher education. Those who have less formal education are also more likely to be poor, adding to the challenge of increasing account ownership among this group.

What are the links with employment status?

Adults who are active in the labor force—either employed or seeking work—are more likely to have an account than those who are out of the labor force. Working adults have many needs for financial services, such as receiving wages from an employer or saving their earnings from a business. Globally, 74 percent of adults who are active in the labor force have an account, while 59 percent of those who are out of the labor force have one, leaving a gap of 15 percentage points (figure 1.18). The gap is similar in developing economies and smaller in high-income ones.

FIGURE 1.18
Account ownership is higher among adults active in the labor force
Adults with an account (%), 2017

Sources: Global Findex database; Gallup World Poll 2017.

FIGURE 1.19
Across a range of economies, adults active in the labor force are more likely to have an account
Adults with an account (%), 2017

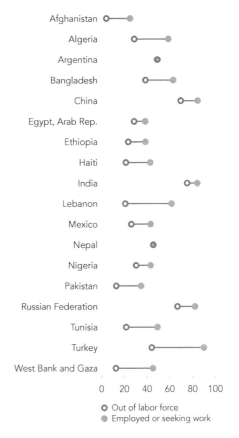

Sources: Global Findex database; Gallup World Poll 2017.

Most developing economies have a gap in account ownership between these two groups. Although account ownership is relatively low overall in Afghanistan, adults who are active in the labor force are roughly six times as likely to have an account as those who are not (figure 1.19). Large gaps between the two groups are found in some economies in the Middle East and North Africa. Compared with adults who are out of the labor force, account ownership among adults who are active in the labor force is roughly twice as high in Algeria, about three times as high in Lebanon, and almost four times as high in West Bank and Gaza. Argentina and Nepal are among the few developing economies with no such gap.

What about the urban-rural gap?

In developing economies account ownership tends to be lower in rural areas than in urban areas. But precisely quantifying the urban-rural gap presents difficulties.

For one thing, distinguishing between urban and rural areas is not straightforward—should the distinction be based solely on population, on the availability of certain services and infrastructure, or on subjective measures such as the judgment of the interviewer or respondent? This is especially challenging in a cross-country context; what might be considered rural in Bangladesh or India, for example, might be considered urban in less populous countries. The Gallup World Poll—the survey to which the Global Findex questionnaire is added—uses different approaches across countries to account for country-specific characteristics, which makes it difficult to create a consistent definition of the urban-rural divide at the global and regional level.

Another challenge is that the estimates of account ownership for urban populations are often imprecise. The Gallup World Poll surveys about 1,000 individuals in most economies, and in those with a predominantly rural population—including many Sub-Saharan African countries—this often means that the number of urban observations is small, resulting in estimates with large margins of error.

Moreover, since 2011 Gallup, Inc., has changed its methodology in a number of countries to improve the within-country geographical representativeness of samples. For some countries this has increased the challenges in making a meaningful comparison of account ownership in rural areas over time. For all these reasons the 2017 Global Findex database provides, in addition to overall nationally representative data on account ownership, estimates for account ownership among rural populations but not urban populations and offers no comparisons with 2011 and 2014 data on rural account ownership at the global or regional level.

China and India are two countries where a consistent methodology does allow comparisons of account ownership among rural dwellers over time. In China the share of adults with an account among this group jumped from 58 percent in 2011 to 77 percent in 2014. India started with lower account ownership among rural adults in 2011, at 33 percent. By 2017 that share had more than doubled—to 79 percent, basically the same as in China.

Notes

1. Data on adults with an account at a financial institution also include respondents who reported having a debit card in their own name. The data also include an additional 3.93 percent of respondents who reported receiving wages, government transfers, a public sector pension, or payments for the sale of agricultural products into a financial institution account in the past 12 months; paying utility bills or school fees from a financial institution account in the past 12 months; or receiving wages or government transfers into a card (which is assumed either to be linked to an account or to support a card-based account) in the past 12 months.

    The definition of formal financial institution used by the Global Findex database encompasses all types of financial institutions that offer deposit, checking, and savings accounts—including banks, credit unions, microfinance institutions, and post offices—and that fall under prudential regulation by a government body. The definition does not include nonbank financial institutions such as pension funds, retirement accounts, insurance companies, or equity holdings such as stocks. As used throughout the report, *financial institution* refers to a formal financial institution.

2. Data on adults with a mobile money account include an additional 0.60 percent of respondents who reported receiving wages, government transfers, a public sector pension, or payments for the sale of agricultural products through a mobile phone in the past 12 months. Unlike for an account at a financial institution, the definition of a mobile money account does not include the payment of utility bills or school fees through a mobile phone; the reason is that the phrasing of the possible answers leaves it open whether those payments were made using a mobile money account or an over-the-counter service.
3. See Demirgüç-Kunt and others (2017).

2 THE UNBANKED

Globally, about 1.7 billion adults remain unbanked—without an account at a financial institution or through a mobile money provider. In 2014 that number was 2 billion.

Because account ownership is nearly universal in high-income economies, virtually all unbanked adults live in developing economies. China and India, despite having relatively high account ownership, claim large shares of the global unbanked population because of their sheer size. Home to 225 million adults without an account, China has the world's largest unbanked population, followed by India (190 million), Pakistan (100 million), and Indonesia (95 million) (map 2.1). Indeed, these four economies, together with three others—Nigeria, Mexico, and Bangladesh—are home to nearly half the world's unbanked population (figure 2.1).

MAP 2.1
Globally, 1.7 billion adults lack an account
Adults without an account, 2017

Source: Global Findex database.
Note: Data are not displayed for economies where the share of adults without an account is 5 percent or less.

FIGURE 2.1

Nearly half of all unbanked adults live in just seven economies

Adults without an account by economy (%), 2017

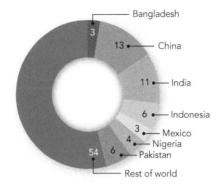

Source: Global Findex database.

Who the unbanked are

Women are overrepresented among the world's unbanked. About 980 million do not have an account, 56 percent of all unbanked adults globally (figure 2.2).

Women are also overrepresented among the unbanked in most economies. This is true even in economies that have successfully increased account ownership and have a relatively small share of adults who are unbanked. In Kenya, where only about a fifth of adults are unbanked, about two-thirds of them are women (figure 2.3). Women make up nearly 60 percent of unbanked adults in China and India—and an even higher share in Turkey. Things are not much different in economies where half or more of adults remain unbanked: in Bangladesh 65 percent of unbanked adults are women, and in Colombia 56 percent are.

Those without an account, men as well as women, tend to be concentrated among poorer households. Globally, about a quarter of unbanked adults live in the poorest 20 percent of households within their economy, about twice the share living in the richest 20 percent (figure 2.4).

Sorting households within each economy into just two groups—the poorest 40 percent and the richest 60 percent—provides another perspective. Worldwide, half of unbanked adults come from the poorest 40 percent of households within their economy, while the other half live in the richest 60 percent. This global pattern is replicated in many economies where half or more of adults are unbanked, such as Colombia, Ethiopia, Indonesia, and Nigeria. In these economies unbanked adults are just as likely to come from poorer households as from wealthier ones.

But in economies that have expanded account ownership to two-thirds or more of adults, poor adults are more overrepresented among the unbanked (figure 2.5). In China, for example, where about a fifth of all adults are unbanked,

Worldwide, most unbanked adults are women

Adults without an account by gender (%), 2017

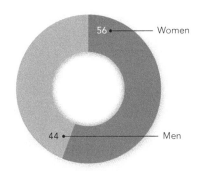

Source: Global Findex database.

Twice as many unbanked adults live in the poorest households in their economy as in the richest ones

Adults without an account by within-economy income quintile (%), 2017

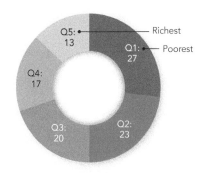

Source: Global Findex database.

Women are overrepresented among the unbanked in most economies

Adults without an account (%), 2017

Economies with a third or less of adults unbanked

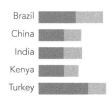

Economies with half or more of adults unbanked

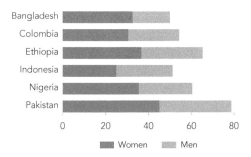

Source: Global Findex database.

In economies where a small share of adults remain unbanked, most of the unbanked are poor

Adults without an account (%), 2017

Economies with a third or less of adults unbanked

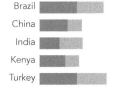

Economies with half or more of adults unbanked

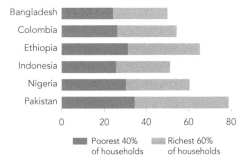

Source: Global Findex database.

FIGURE 2.6

Three in 10 unbanked adults are between the ages of 15 and 24

Adults without an account by age group (%), 2017

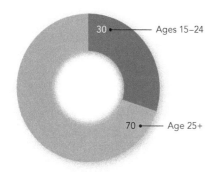

Source: Global Findex database.

65 percent of this group belongs to the poorest 40 percent of households. In Brazil, where a little less than a third of adults are unbanked, 58 percent of these adults live in the poorest 40 percent of households.

Unbanked adults are disproportionately young. Globally, 30 percent of unbanked adults are between 15 and 24 years old (figure 2.6).[1] Among all adults in developing economies, only 23 percent fall in that age group. The unbanked population is even younger in economies where the share of unbanked adults is relatively small. In Brazil, India, and Kenya about 4 in 10 unbanked adults are in the age group 15–24.

Unbanked adults tend to have low educational attainment. Globally, 62 percent of the unbanked have a primary education or less, compared with about half of adults overall in developing economies. This share is even higher in some economies, such as Ethiopia, where 92 percent of unbanked adults have a primary education or less —as well as Tanzania (86 percent) and Pakistan (75 percent). Worldwide, only 38 percent of the unbanked have completed high school or postsecondary education (figure 2.7).

A slight majority of unbanked adults are either employed or seeking work. Yet compared with other adults, those who are unbanked are more likely to be out of the labor force. Among all adults in developing economies, 37 percent are out of the labor force. Among unbanked adults, that share is 10 percentage points higher (figure 2.8).

FIGURE 2.7

Most unbanked adults have a primary education or less

Adults without an account by educational attainment (%), 2017

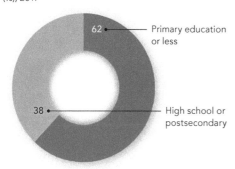

Source: Global Findex database.

FIGURE 2.8

Almost half of unbanked adults are out of the labor force

Adults without an account by labor force participation (%), 2017

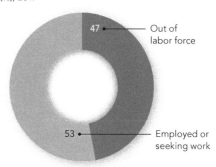

Sources: Global Findex database; Gallup World Poll 2017.

FIGURE 2.9
Among the unbanked, women are less likely than men to participate in the labor force
Adults without an account by gender and labor force participation (%), 2017

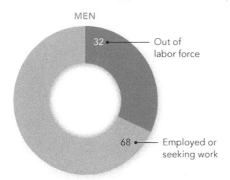

MEN

32 — Out of labor force

68 — Employed or seeking work

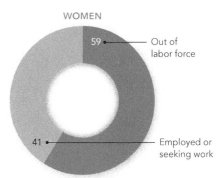

WOMEN

59 — Out of labor force

41 — Employed or seeking work

Sources: Global Findex database; Gallup World Poll 2017.

These global numbers obscure gender inequality in labor force participation among unbanked adults. The majority of unbanked men—68 percent—are employed or seeking work. For unbanked women the picture is flipped: 59 percent are out of the labor force altogether (figure 2.9).

Among unbanked adults who are economically active, self-employment is the most common form of work. Indeed, more than a quarter of all unbanked adults reported being self-employed, while less than a fifth reported working for wages (figure 2.10). The reverse is true for adults overall in the developing world: the share working for wages, at 31 percent, is slightly larger than the share who are self-employed.

FIGURE 2.10
Self-employment is the most common form of work for unbanked adults
Adults without an account by employment status (%), 2017

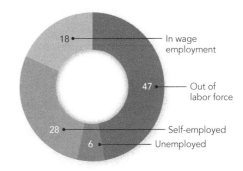

18 — In wage employment

47 — Out of labor force

28 — Self-employed

6 — Unemployed

Sources: Global Findex database; Gallup World Poll 2017.

Why people remain unbanked

Globally, 31 percent of adults are unbanked. To help shed light on the reasons for this, the 2017 Global Findex survey asked adults without an account at a financial institution why they do not have one. Respondents could offer more than one reason, and most gave two.

The most commonly cited barrier was lack of enough money. Nearly two-thirds of adults without an account at a financial institution said that they have too little money to use one, and roughly one in five cited this as their sole reason

FIGURE 2.11

Lack of enough money is the most commonly cited barrier to account ownership

Adults without a financial institution account reporting barrier as a reason for not having one (%), 2017

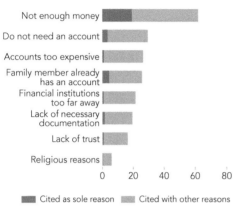

Source: Global Findex database.
Note: Respondents could choose more than one reason.

for not having one (figure 2.11). No other reason was cited as the sole barrier by more than 5 percent.

Worldwide, 30 percent of adults without an account at a financial institution said that they do not need one, making this the second most common reason cited. Yet only 3 percent cited it as their only reason for not having an account. This suggests that among those reporting lack of need as one of several reasons, some might be open to using financial services if the services are accessible and relevant to their lives.

Cost is another important barrier, cited by 26 percent of adults without an account at a financial institution. But the share reporting that accounts are too expensive was twice as high in Latin America and the Caribbean. In Brazil, Colombia, and Peru almost 60 percent cited cost as a barrier.

A similar global share, 26 percent, said that they do not have an account because a family member already has one. In some economies women were more likely than men to cite this reason. Among those without an account in Turkey, 72 percent of women mentioned this reason, while 51 percent of men did. In China the share for women was 35 percent, and for men 27 percent.

Distance is a barrier for many: 22 percent of adults without an account said that financial institutions are too far away. In some economies the share was higher, with about 33 percent citing distance as a barrier in Brazil, Indonesia, and Kenya—and 41 percent doing so in the Philippines.

Documentation requirements also hamper account ownership. Twenty percent of adults without an account at a financial institution reported lacking the documentation needed to open one. Higher shares cited this barrier in such economies as Zambia (35 percent), the Philippines (45 percent), and Zimbabwe (49 percent).

Distrust in the financial system features as a greater barrier in some regions than in others. Globally, 16 percent of adults without an account at a financial institution cited this barrier—but the share was more than twice as high in Europe and Central Asia and in Latin America and the Caribbean.

While only 6 percent of adults without an account at a financial institution cited religious concerns as a reason, the share was substantially higher in some economies with a predominantly Muslim population. In Pakistan 13 percent mentioned religious reasons, and in Turkey 19 percent did. Yet high costs turned out to be at least as important as religious concerns in each of these economies —cited by 21 percent in Pakistan and 19 percent in Turkey. And the share who reported religious concerns as their sole reason for not having an account was minuscule—2 percent in Pakistan and 1 percent in Turkey. Moreover, in several other economies with a mostly Muslim population—including Bangladesh, the Arab Republic of Egypt, and Indonesia—the share citing religious reasons was virtually the same as the world average.[2]

Notes

1. This share does not change if young adults are defined as those ages 18–24.
2. The low share of adults without an account at a financial institution citing religious concerns as a reason in some economies with a predominantly Muslim population could reflect the presence of Sharia-compliant financial institutions in these economies.

3 PAYMENTS

Most people make payments—such as for utility bills or domestic remittances. And most receive payments—such as wages, other payments for work, or government transfers. The 2017 Global Findex survey asked people what kinds of payments they make and receive and how they carry out these transactions—whether using an account or in cash.

The Global Findex survey asked questions about nine types of payments that can be grouped into five broad categories: *payments from government to people* (public sector wages, public sector pensions, and government transfers); *payments from businesses to people* (private sector wages); *other payments for work* (payments for the sale of agricultural products and payments from self-employment); *payments from people to businesses* (utility payments); and *payments between people* (domestic remittances, both those sent and those received). In developing economies the survey collected data on all nine types of payments. But in most high-income economies, because of time limits on interviews conducted by phone, the survey collected data only on government payments, private sector wage payments, payments from self-employment, and utility payments.[1]

This chapter distinguishes mainly between payments using an account and payments in cash only.[2] For domestic remittances it also distinguishes one additional payment channel: using an over-the-counter (OTC) service. This involves a transaction completed in cash at a financial service provider, which transfers the money digitally on behalf of the sender and recipient.

Some people who reported sending or receiving a payment, when asked about the payment channel used, provided a response of "no," "don't know," or "refuse" to all possible options. These respondents, typically representing only a small share of adults in any economy, are reported as those using some other method. This category could include people making or receiving payments by check.

Payments from government to people

Globally, 23 percent of adults reported having received at least one payment from the government in the past year—in the form of public sector wages, a public sector pension, or government transfers. Government transfers include any kind of social benefits—such as subsidies, unemployment benefits, or payments for educational or medical expenses. Not surprisingly, the share of adults receiving government payments is about twice as high in high-income economies (43 percent) as in developing ones (19 percent). And among developing economies, the share in upper-middle-income economies (24 percent) is about twice the share in low- and lower-middle-income ones.

FIGURE 3.1

Except in low-income economies, most people getting government payments receive them into an account

Adults receiving government payments in the past year (%), 2017

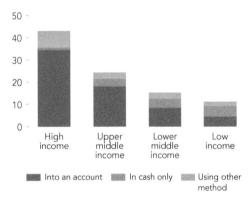

Source: Global Findex database.

How do people receive government payments?

In high-income economies the overwhelming majority (80 percent) of those getting government payments receive them into an account (figure 3.1). Another 21 percent reported receiving such payments in some other way than into an account or in cash, probably in the form of either checks or vouchers.[3] Among developing economies, the most common way of receiving government payments varies by income classification. In upper-middle-income economies 74 percent of recipients reported receiving government payments into an account—a majority almost as large as that in high-income economies. In lower-middle-income economies just over half (55 percent) reported receiving the payments this way, and in low-income economies 39 percent did.

Among developing regions, Europe and Central Asia has a particularly high share of adults receiving government payments. Indeed, this share is about twice the average for developing economies, driven by the large numbers receiving public sector wage or pension payments. In Kazakhstan and the Russian Federation, for example, more than 30 percent of adults reported having received government payments, and more than two-thirds of them said that they received the payments into an account (figure 3.2).

Government payments to people play an important part in other developing economies as well. These include Brazil, Indonesia, the Philippines, and South Africa, where 20 percent or more of adults reported receiving such payments. But while about 80 percent of the recipients in Brazil and South Africa receive the payments into an account, those in Indonesia are about equally likely to receive them into an account or in cash. And in the Philippines the majority

FIGURE 3.2

In most developing economies governments make payments to people primarily into accounts

Adults receiving government payments in the past year (%), 2017

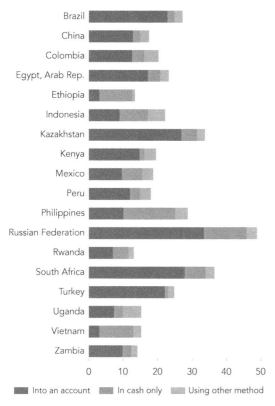

Into an account   In cash only   Using other method

Source: Global Findex database.

receive the payments in cash. The same is true in Ethiopia and Vietnam, for example. In most developing economies, however, government payments to people are made primarily into accounts.

What are the patterns for different types of government payments?

The focus so far has been on overall government payments to people. What does a more detailed look at the data reveal? In developing economies on average, 4 percent of adults reported having received public sector wages in the past 12 months, 7 percent a public sector pension, and 12 percent government transfers. (Because people may receive more than one type of government payment, the sum of these percentages is larger than the overall share who reported having received government payments in the past year.) The corresponding averages in high-income economies are 11 percent for public sector wages, 18 percent for public sector pensions, and 23 percent for government transfers.

FIGURE 3.3

Some European and Central Asian economies have a particularly high share of adults receiving public sector wages

Adults receiving public sector wages in the past year (%), 2017

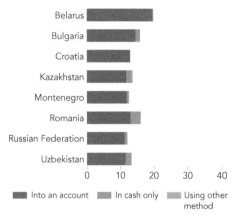

Source: Global Findex database.

FIGURE 3.4

Government transfers are important in some developing economies—and paid mostly into accounts

Adults receiving government transfers in the past year (%), 2017

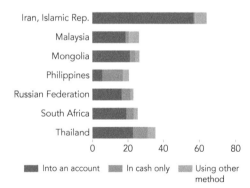

Source: Global Findex database.

Among high-income economies, Norway and Sweden both have a notably high share of adults (up to 25 percent) reporting public sector wage payments. Beyond high-income economies, some of the highest shares can be found in Europe and Central Asia (figure 3.3).[4] In Russia 12 percent of adults reported having received public sector wage payments, and in Belarus 20 percent did so. Public sector wages are paid almost exclusively into accounts in these economies. This pattern holds across economies: globally, less than 1 percent of adults reported having received public sector wages only in cash.

With the high share of adults in public sector employment in high-income economies and many European and Central Asian economies, it is no surprise that these economies also have a particularly high share receiving a public sector pension. In Russia 29 percent of adults reported having received a public sector pension in the past 12 months. Among other major developing economies, a much smaller share did so in Brazil, China, and India, only 6–7 percent. But in South Africa 19 percent of adults reported having received a public sector pension in the past 12 months—one of only six economies outside Europe and Central Asia and the high-income group where the share exceeds 10 percent.[5] Unlike for public sector wages, about a third of those receiving a public sector pension in Russia reported receiving the payments in cash. Globally on average, 16 percent of those receiving a public sector pension said that they received it in cash.

Government transfer payments play an important part in many economies around the world. The share of adults receiving government transfers is predictably large in high-income economies, 23 percent on average. Among developing economies the share ranges from less than 5 percent in some to as high as 64 percent in the Islamic Republic of Iran, which has a national unconditional cash transfer program (figure 3.4). In a handful of developing economies about 20 percent or more of adults receive such payments. And while most transfer recipients receive the payments into an account, the Philippines is among the few economies where most receive the payments in cash.

What do the data show about government payment recipients within economies? Notably, poorer and richer adults are about equally likely to receive government payments, in high-income and developing economies alike (figure 3.5). Moreover, they are equally likely to receive such payments into an account. And for all three types of government payments—public sector wages, public sector pensions, and government transfers—poorer and richer adults are about equally likely to be recipients.

Payments from businesses to people—private sector wages

Globally, 28 percent of adults reported having received at least one wage payment from a private sector employer in the past year—46 percent of adults in high-income economies and 24 percent in developing ones. In high-income economies 85 percent of these wage earners reported receiving their wage payments into an account, while in developing economies only about half did so (46 percent).

But these averages mask variation within these two groups of economies. Among high-income economies, while the overwhelming majority of adults earning private sector wages reported receiving the payments into an account, there are still some differences. Take the Group of Seven (G-7) economies, for example. In Germany and the United Kingdom virtually all those receiving private sector wages reported being paid directly into an account (figure 3.6). In Japan, by contrast, 13 percent of private sector wage earners—or 7 percent of all adults—reported being paid in cash. And in Canada, France, Italy, and the United States about 5 percent of all adults reported receiving private sector wages in some other way—probably by check.

Not surprisingly, there are even more pronounced differences among developing economies, both in the share of adults receiving private sector wages and in how they receive these payments. For example, in Brazil, China, Russia, and South Africa—all upper-middle-income economies—between 60 and 70 percent of private sector wage earners reported receiving their wage payments into an account (figure 3.7). In Kenya, a lower-middle-income economy, a similarly large share

FIGURE 3.5

Poorer adults are as likely as richer ones to receive government payments—and to do so into an account

Adults receiving government payments in the past year (%), 2017

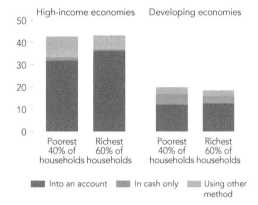

Source: Global Findex database.
Note: Data for the poorest 40 percent and richest 60 percent of households are based on household income quintiles within economies.

FIGURE 3.6

In most G-7 economies virtually all private sector wage earners are paid into an account

Adults receiving private sector wages in the past year (%), 2017

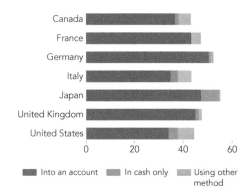

Source: Global Findex database.

reported being paid into an account. By contrast, in four other lower-middle-income economies —the Arab Republic of Egypt, India, Indonesia, and Nigeria—where the average share of adults receiving private sector wages is smaller, most reported being paid in cash, much as in Ethiopia, a low-income economy. And in Mexico, despite its being an upper-middle-income economy, private sector wage earners were about equally likely to report receiving wage payments into an account or in cash, while about 20 percent reported receiving them in some other way.

In developing economies women were about half as likely as men to report receiving private sector wages (figure 3.8). In high-income economies, by contrast, women were only moderately less likely than men to do so. But in developing and high-income economies alike, women earning private sector wages were just as likely as their male counterparts to report receiving their wage payments into an account.

FIGURE 3.7

How private sector wage earners are most likely to receive their pay varies across developing economies

Adults receiving private sector wages in the past year (%), 2017

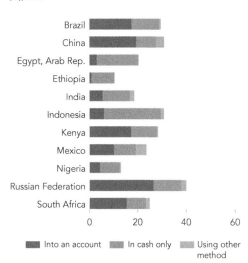

Source: Global Findex database.

FIGURE 3.8

Women are as likely as men to receive their private sector wages into an account

Adults receiving private sector wages in the past year (%), 2017

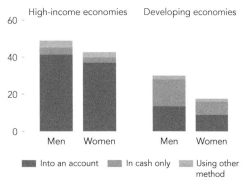

Source: Global Findex database.

Other payments for work

Around the world, most people getting paid for their labor receive the payments in the form of a salary or wages from an employer, whether in the public or private sector. But some receive other payments for work, such as from the sale of agricultural products or from self-employment.

How do people receive payments for agricultural products?

About 15 percent of adults in developing economies reported having received payments for the sale of agricultural products in the past 12 months. Most said that they received these payments in cash—on average across developing regions, only one in five recipients of agricultural payments reported receiving them into an account. But in Sub-Saharan Africa, where the share receiving agricultural payments is about twice the average for developing economies, a much higher share of recipients reported receiving such payments into an account in some economies. Indeed, in Ghana, Kenya, and Zambia about 40 percent of recipients, and in Uganda 32 percent—more than 10 percent of all adults in these countries—reported receiving agricultural payments into an account, in most cases a mobile money account (figure 3.9).

How do people receive payments from self-employment?

In 2017, for the first time, the Global Findex survey asked respondents who reported receiving neither wage payments nor agricultural payments whether they had received payments from self-employment in the past 12 months. These include payments from their business, from selling goods, or from providing services, including part-time work. About 8 percent of adults in both high-income and developing economies reported having received such payments in the past year. But while about two-thirds of recipients in high-income economies reported receiving the payments into an account, only about a quarter did so in developing economies. Still, there are some exceptions. In Kenya, Mongolia, and South Africa, for example, about half of those receiving payments from self-employment said that they received them directly into an account (figure 3.10).

FIGURE 3.9

In most developing economies, though not all, agricultural payments are received mainly in cash

Adults receiving payments for agricultural products in the past year (%), 2017

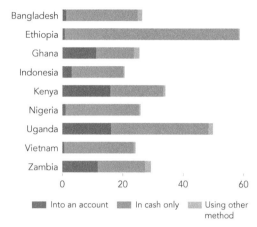

Source: Global Findex database.

FIGURE 3.10

Those earning money from self-employment in developing economies are paid mostly in cash

Adults receiving payments from self-employment in the past year (%), 2017

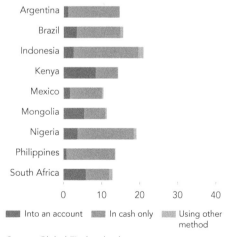

Source: Global Findex database.

Payments from people to businesses—utility payments

Worldwide, 57 percent of adults reported having made regular payments for water, electricity, or trash collection in the past 12 months. In high-income economies 77 percent reported making such payments. In developing economies 53 percent did so, with the share ranging from 28 percent in Sub-Saharan Africa to around 70 percent in East Asia and the Pacific and Europe and Central Asia.

FIGURE 3.11

One in four people paying utility bills in developing economies does so directly from an account
Adults paying utility bills in the past year (%), 2017

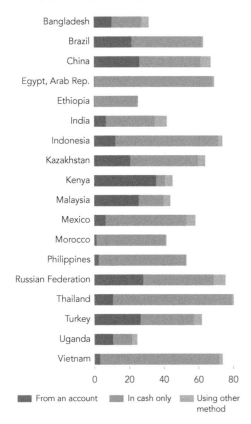

From an account ▪ In cash only ▪ Using other method

Source: Global Findex database.

In high-income economies the vast majority of those making utility payments reported doing so directly from an account; in developing economies only about a quarter said this (figure 3.11). Yet there is wide variation across developing economies. In Egypt, Ethiopia, Morocco, the Philippines, and Vietnam, for example, virtually everyone making utility payments does so in cash. But a majority of those in Kenya and Malaysia pay directly from an account—as do about 40 percent in China, Russia, Turkey, and Uganda.

Payments between people—domestic remittances

Domestic remittances are an important part of the economy in many places.[6] In developing economies on average, 27 percent of adults reported having used domestic remittances in the past 12 months—either sending money to or receiving it from a relative or friend living in another area of their country.[7] Domestic remittances are particularly important in Sub-Saharan Africa, where 45 percent on average reported having sent or received such payments.[8] Gabon, Ghana, Kenya, Namibia, and Uganda have the highest shares of adults using domestic remittances, about 60–70 percent (figure 3.12). Outside Sub-Saharan Africa, only Cambodia, the Dominican Republic, Mongolia, the Philippines, and Thailand have shares exceeding 40 percent.

People send and receive domestic remittances in different ways, including by using an account and in cash only. In addition to these payment channels, this section also considers the use of an over-the-counter service, such as at a money transfer service like Western Union. OTC services for domestic remittances are also offered by financial institutions and mobile money operators. Payments are classified as OTC if the sender or recipient did not use an account but instead transacted in cash at the service provider, which transferred the funds electronically on his or her behalf. Domestic remittances are therefore considered to have been sent or received through an OTC service if the sender or recipient reported either using a money transfer service or using a financial institution or mobile money operator but did not report having an account.

In developing economies the most common way of sending or receiving domestic remittances is by using an account. On average in these economies, 46 percent of adults who reported having sent or received domestic remittances in the past year said that they used this method—while 27 percent reported using cash only, 19 percent using an OTC service, and 8 percent using some other method.[9] This pattern generally holds, including on average for economies in Sub-Saharan Africa. But in some economies people are most likely to use cash, and in still others they are most likely to use an OTC service.

Kenya has the highest share using an account: among adults sending or receiving domestic remittances in the past year, 89 percent reported having used an account to do so, in most cases a mobile money account. This should come as no surprise—because when the mobile money operator M-PESA launched its business in Kenya in 2007, it specifically targeted the domestic remittances market, promoting its services with the slogan "send money home." Indeed, among those sending or receiving at least one domestic remittance payment in Sub-Saharan Africa, most reported having done so through a mobile phone —through either a mobile money account or an OTC service. But in some economies, including Ethiopia, Namibia, Nigeria, and South Africa, people sending domestic remittances through an account are most likely to do so using an account at a bank or another type of financial institution. In Cambodia and the Philippines, by contrast, the most common way to send or receive domestic remittances is by using an OTC service. And in Egypt and India the most common way is by using cash only.

FIGURE 3.12

In Sub-Saharan Africa domestic remittances are particularly important— and are sent and received mainly by using an account

Adults sending or receiving domestic remittances in the past year (%), 2017

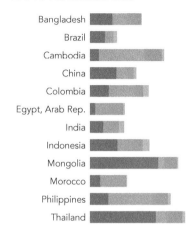

Outside Sub-Saharan Africa

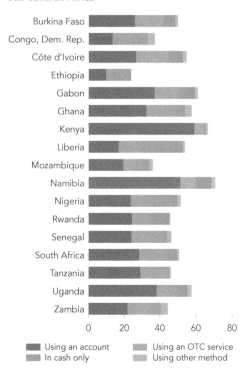

Source: Global Findex database.

Notes

1. Gallup, Inc., imposes a time limit on phone interviews, the typical survey method used in high-income economies, which limits the number of Global Findex survey questions that can be added to the Gallup World Poll core questionnaire. In 13 high-income economies included in the 2017 Global Findex database, however, Gallup, Inc., conducts face-to-face rather than phone interviews, and in these economies data were collected for all nine types of payments. And in 4 developing economies included in the database, Gallup, Inc., conducts interviews by phone, similarly limiting the number of questions that could be added.

2. Payments are considered to have been received into an account if the respondent reported receiving them directly into an account at a financial institution; into a card, which is assumed either to be linked to an account or to support a card-based account; or through a mobile phone—and they are considered to have been sent from an account if the respondent reported sending them directly from a financial institution account or through a mobile phone. However, a payment to or from a mobile phone is considered a payment into or from an account only if the respondent lives in an economy where mobile money accounts are provided by a service that was in the GSM Association's Mobile Money for the Unbanked (GSMA MMU) database at the time of the survey.

3. Less than 1 percent of adults in both high-income and developing economies reported having received government payments both into an account and in cash. The reason could be that they received more than one type of government payment, with one being paid into an account and another being paid in cash. Because these adults reported having received at least one payment into an account, they are included in the category of those receiving payments into an account. (A similar principle applies to other types of payments discussed in this chapter.)

4. Outside Europe and Central Asia, the only developing economies with a comparable share of adults receiving public sector wages are the Dominican Republic (11 percent), Libya (13 percent), Mauritius (12 percent), and Namibia (16 percent).

5. The other five economies are Costa Rica (11 percent), the Islamic Republic of Iran (11 percent), Jordan (12 percent), Mauritius (22 percent), and Namibia (11 percent).

6. The Global Findex survey does not cover international remittances. While international remittances are economically important for some economies, the share of adults in developing economies who reported sending or receiving them is on average 4 percent (Gallup World Poll 2017).

7. In developing economies 17 percent of adults reported having sent domestic remittances in the past 12 months, and 20 percent having received them; 9 percent of adults reported having both sent and received domestic remittances.

8. In Sub-Saharan Africa 28 percent of adults reported having sent domestic remittances in the past 12 months, and 33 percent having received them; 17 percent of adults reported having both sent and received domestic remittances.

9. Respondents who reported sending or receiving domestic remittances in multiple ways are assigned to categories as follows: *using an account* if they reported having sent or received domestic remittances through an account; *using an OTC service* if they reported having sent or received domestic remittances through an OTC service but did not report having done so through an account; *in cash only* if they reported having sent or received domestic remittances only in cash; and *using other method* if they provided a "no," "don't know," or "refuse" response to all categories.

4 USE OF ACCOUNTS

Owning an account is an important first step toward financial inclusion. But to fully benefit from having an account, people need to be able to use it in safe and convenient ways. This chapter explores different ways in which people access and use their accounts.

Use of accounts for digital payments

According to the 2017 Global Findex survey, 52 percent of adults—or 76 percent of account owners—around the world reported making or receiving at least one digital payment in the past year (figure 4.1). In high-income economies 91 percent of adults (97 percent of account owners) reported doing so; in developing economies 44 percent of adults (70 percent of account owners) did. These percentages include all respondents who reported using mobile money, a debit or credit card, or a mobile phone to make a payment from an account, or reported using the internet to pay bills or to buy something online, in the past 12 months. They also include those who reported paying bills, sending or receiving remittances, receiving payments for agricultural products, or receiving wages, government transfers, or a public sector pension directly from or into a financial institution account or through a mobile money account in the past 12 months.[1]

What are the overall changes since 2014?

The use of digital payments is on the rise. Between 2014 and 2017 the share of adults around the world making or receiving digital payments rose by 11 percentage points, from 41 percent to 52 percent (see figure 4.1).[2] Indeed, the growth in the share using digital payments outpaced the growth in the share owning an account, which hit 7 percentage points. In developing economies the share using digital payments increased by 12 percentage points—from 32 percent to 44 percent—among all adults, while it grew from 57 percent to 70 percent among account owners. In high-income economies the use of digital payments was already nearly universal among account owners in 2014, and it remained so.

While the use of digital payments is generally high in developing economies— reported by more than two-thirds of account owners on average—there is also

FIGURE 4.1

More people are using their account to make or receive digital payments
Adults with an account (%)

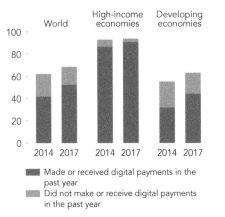

- ■ Made or received digital payments in the past year
- ▦ Did not make or receive digital payments in the past year

Source: Global Findex database.

FIGURE 4.2

The share of account owners using digital payments varies widely across developing economies
Adults with an account (%), 2017

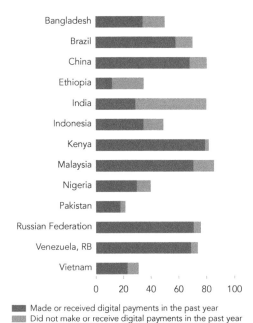

- ■ Made or received digital payments in the past year
- ▦ Did not make or receive digital payments in the past year

Source: Global Findex database.

much variation among these economies (figure 4.2). In Kenya, thanks to the widespread adoption of mobile money accounts, the use of digital payments is nearly universal among account owners; indeed, the share reporting their use, at 97 percent, is as high as that in high-income economies. In the Russian Federation and República Bolivariana de Venezuela the share of account owners using digital payments is similarly high, and in China it is 85 percent. By contrast, Ethiopia and India stand out for low use of digital payments: only about a third of account owners in these two countries reported making or receiving at least one digital payment in the past 12 months.[3]

What do the data show about the use of digital payments in major developing economies that already had a high rate of account ownership in 2014? These include Brazil, China, Kenya, Malaysia, Russia, South Africa, and Thailand, where the share of adults with an account had reached about 70 percent or more. While account ownership remained largely unchanged in these countries, the share of adults using their account for digital payments generally grew substantially. In China, for example, the share of adults using digital payments increased by about half, from 44 percent in 2014 to 68 percent in 2017 (figure 4.3). In Thailand the share almost doubled, to 62 percent. Economies such as Brazil, Malaysia, and Russia also saw increases, though much more modest ones from a larger base. In Kenya and South Africa the share of account owners using digital payments had already surpassed 85 percent in 2014.

Does the use of accounts for digital payments vary by gender and by income? As explored in the chapter on account ownership, women and poorer adults are less likely to have an account. But does the use of accounts vary among those who do have one?

Among account owners in high-income economies, the use of digital payments is nearly universal for both men and women. Among those in developing economies, however, men are on average 5 percentage points more likely than women to make or receive digital payments—72 percent of male account owners use digital payments, compared with 67 percent of female account owners. This gender gap of 5 percentage points remains unchanged since 2014 despite an overall increase in the use of digital payments.

The gender gap in the use of digital payments varies substantially among developing economies. In some it reaches double digits. These include economies that also have a double-digit gender gap in account ownership, such as Bangladesh, the Arab Republic of Egypt, Ethiopia, Morocco, and Pakistan. By contrast, in Turkey, despite a gender gap in account ownership of almost 30 percentage points, the use of digital payments is nearly universal among both male and female account owners. Conversely, a double-digit gender gap in the use of digital payments also exists in some economies that have a smaller gender gap in account ownership. In India, for example, 42 percent of male account owners use digital payments, while just 29 percent of female account owners do. And in the Philippines, one of the few developing economies where women are more likely than men to have an account, the share of account owners using digital payments is 9 percentage points higher among men than among women.

FIGURE 4.3

In developing economies where most adults already had an account, a growing share are using theirs for digital payments
Adults with an account (%)

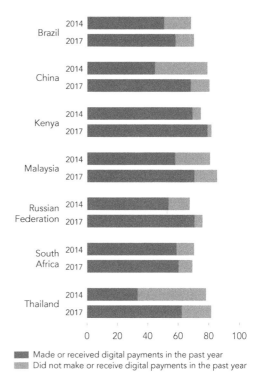

■ Made or received digital payments in the past year
▨ Did not make or receive digital payments in the past year

Source: Global Findex database.

Not surprisingly, there are also differences between richer and poorer account owners in the share using digital payments. Globally, 80 percent of account owners living in the richest 60 percent of households within economies make or receive digital payments, while 70 percent of those in the poorest 40 percent of households do so. In high-income economies richer and poorer account owners are equally likely to use digital payments. In developing economies, by contrast, 74 percent of richer adults use digital payments, while 61 percent of poorer adults do. The gap between richer and poorer in the use of accounts for digital payments has narrowed by a third since 2014, when it was 22 percentage points on average in developing economies and 15 percentage points globally.

Payment cards such as debit or credit cards provide account owners a convenient way to make payments from their account without having to withdraw cash. In high-income economies 80 percent of adults reported using a debit or credit card to make at least one payment in the past 12 months, while in developing economies only 22 percent did so (figure 4.4).[4]

FIGURE 4.4

In high-income economies four-fifths of adults use a debit or credit card
Adults with an account (%), 2017

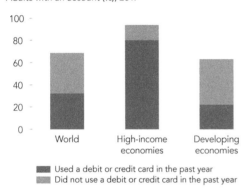

Used a debit or credit card in the past year
Did not use a debit or credit card in the past year

Source: Global Findex database.

People can use a debit card both to make direct payments from their account and to withdraw money from it through an automated teller machine (ATM) rather than a bank teller. In high-income economies on average, 89 percent of account owners (83 percent of adults) reported owning a debit card in 2017, and three-quarters of account owners said that they had used their card to make a direct purchase in the past 12 months (figure 4.5). In developing economies only 63 percent of account owners (40 percent of adults) said that they had a debit card, and just half of them reported using it to make a direct purchase in the past year. While debit card ownership and use have grown in developing economies since 2014, they have done so only modestly: The share of account owners with a debit card has increased by only 5 percentage points, from 58 percent to 63 percent. And the share using a debit card for a direct purchase has similarly increased by only 5 percentage points.[5]

FIGURE 4.5

Debit card ownership and use have grown in developing economies, though slowly
Adults with an account (%)

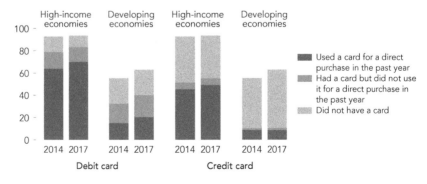

Used a card for a direct purchase in the past year
Had a card but did not use it for a direct purchase in the past year
Did not have a card

Source: Global Findex database.

Debit card ownership and use vary considerably across developing economies (figure 4.6). Brazil, China, Malaysia, Russia, and Turkey follow the general pattern among developing economies of relatively high debit card ownership and use, with about half of those with a debit card using it to make a direct purchase in the past year. In India and Kenya, by contrast, less than half of account owners have a debit card, and among those who do, only about a third used it to make a direct purchase. And in such economies as Egypt, Indonesia, Nigeria, and the Philippines the number of account owners with a debit card is relatively high, but only a third or fewer of those who have one used it for a direct purchase. República Bolivariana de Venezuela stands out for very high debit card ownership and use—nearly universal among adults. A key reason is that the country's economic challenges have led to a severe shortage of bank notes, so that out of necessity many people making a purchase use a debit card whenever possible.[6]

In many economies people use a credit card rather than a debit card to pay bills and make everyday purchases.[7] In high-income economies 55 percent of adults reported owning a credit card. In developing economies, despite recent growth in some, credit card ownership remains low and unchanged from 2014: on average only 10 percent of adults reported having one.

Those who own a credit card are very likely to use it. Across both high-income and developing economies the share of credit card holders who reported having used their card in the past 12 months exceeds 80 percent.

Where are payments using a mobile phone or the internet catching on?

Mobile phones and the internet increasingly offer an alternative way to make direct payments from an account—either a mobile money account or, through an app or a website, a financial institution account. In high-income economies 51 percent of adults (55 percent of account owners) reported making at least one financial transaction in the past year using a mobile phone or the internet.[8] But this average masks a large variation: in Norway the share was as high as 85 percent while it was just 33 percent in Japan and 22 percent in Italy (figure 4.7).

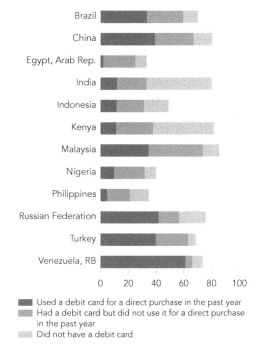

FIGURE 4.6

Debit card ownership and use vary widely among developing economies
Adults with an account (%), 2017

Used a debit card for a direct purchase in the past year
Had a debit card but did not use it for a direct purchase in the past year
Did not have a debit card

Source: Global Findex database.

FIGURE 4.7

Half of adults in high-income economies use a mobile phone or the internet to make transactions from their account
Adults with an account (%), 2017

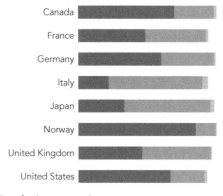

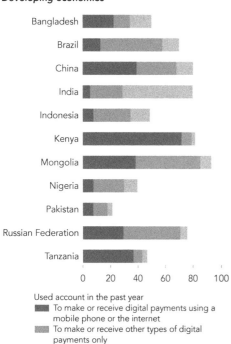

Source: Global Findex database.

In developing economies 19 percent of adults (30 percent of account owners) reported making at least one financial transaction in the past year using a mobile money account, a mobile phone, or the internet. But this figure similarly masks large differences. In economies where a large share of adults have a mobile money account, such as Kenya and Tanzania, the use of a mobile phone to make transactions through an account is close to universal among account owners—in Kenya 88 percent of account owners (72 percent of adults) reported using a mobile phone or the internet to make a transaction through their account in the past year. By contrast, in India less than 10 percent of account owners reported doing so. In China 49 percent of account owners (40 percent of adults) reported using a mobile phone to make a financial transaction.

When it comes to using a mobile phone for financial services, China and Kenya represent two different models. In China mobile financial services are provided primarily through third-party payment service providers such as Alipay and WeChat using smartphone apps linked to an account at a bank or another type of financial institution (figure 4.8). By contrast, in Kenya mobile financial services are offered by mobile network operators, and mobile money accounts do not need to be linked to an account at a financial institution.

In Kenya most account owners have both a financial institution account and a mobile money account. This is reflected in how people make mobile payments. Forty percent of adults use only a mobile money account to make such payments. Another 29 percent rely on two methods—using a mobile money account and using a mobile phone or the internet to access their financial institution account. And 2 percent make mobile payments only by using a mobile phone or the internet to access their financial institution account. In China 40 percent of adults make mobile payments from their financial institution account.

FIGURE 4.8

Account owners in China tend to make mobile payments through apps, those in Kenya through mobile money accounts

Adults with an account (%), 2017

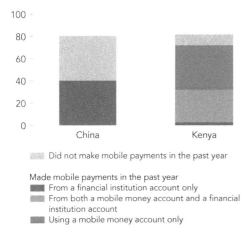

Did not make mobile payments in the past year

Made mobile payments in the past year
■ From a financial institution account only
■ From both a mobile money account and a financial institution account
■ Using a mobile money account only

Source: Global Findex database.
Note: Data on the use of mobile money accounts include adults making or receiving payments through such accounts.

FIGURE 4.9

More than half of adults in high-income economies use a mobile phone or the internet to check the balance in their financial institution account

Adults with a financial institution account (%), 2017

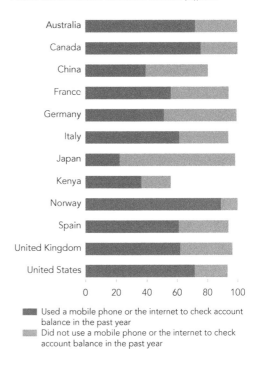

■ Used a mobile phone or the internet to check account balance in the past year
■ Did not use a mobile phone or the internet to check account balance in the past year

Source: Global Findex database.

In 2017, for the first time, the Global Findex survey also asked respondents with a financial institution account whether they used a mobile phone or the internet to check their account balance. In high-income economies 56 percent of adults reported having done so, including almost 90 percent of adults in Norway (figure 4.9). In developing economies on average, 18 percent of adults reported having used a mobile phone or the internet to check their balance. But in a handful of economies about twice that share reported having done so. For example, in China 39 percent of adults did so, and in Kenya 32 percent did. And in Mongolia and Russia about 45 percent did so, the largest share among developing economies.

Most people who use a mobile phone or the internet for checking their account balance also use this technology for making transactions from their financial institution account. But this is not true everywhere: Italy and Spain are two notable exceptions. In these two countries 61 percent of adults reported using a mobile phone or the internet to check the balance in their financial institution account, but less than half of this group also reported doing so to make a transaction from their financial institution account.

Globally, 22 percent of adults reported using the internet to pay bills in the past 12 months, and 24 percent using it to buy something online. Overall, 29 percent of adults around the world reported using the internet to either pay bills or buy something online—68 percent of adults in high-income economies and 21 percent in developing economies.

In high-income economies the share of adults who reported having used the internet to pay bills averages 52 percent—but it exceeds 80 percent in Denmark, Finland, the Netherlands, Norway, and Sweden (figure 4.10). In developing economies few adults use the internet to pay bills. The highest shares doing so—about 40 percent—are in Belarus, China, Croatia, and the Islamic Republic of Iran (figure 4.11). In Russia and Turkey about a third of adults pay bills online. But on average in developing economies only 16 percent of adults do so, and the share is less than 5 percent in low- and lower-middle-income economies.

Similarly, high-income economies have a larger share of adults who reported having used the internet to buy something online in the past year—59 percent on average, including up to three-quarters of adults in Denmark, the Netherlands, Norway, and the United Kingdom. In China 45 percent of adults reported having bought something online—by far the largest share among developing economies. Malaysia followed, with 34 percent. In Belarus, Croatia, the Islamic Republic of Iran, and Russia just under 30 percent of adults reported having made online purchases, and in Turkey and Vietnam about 20 percent did. On average, however, just 7 percent of adults in developing economies excluding China reported having bought something online.

Buying something online does not necessarily mean paying for it online. In many developing economies people commonly pay in cash on delivery for internet orders. To measure how common that practice is, the 2017 Global Findex survey asked people in developing economies how they pay for internet purchases. On average in all developing economies except China, 53 percent of adults who reported making an internet purchase in the past 12 months said that they paid for it in cash on delivery. Even in economies where a relatively large share of adults reported having made an online purchase, such as Malaysia and Turkey, only about half of them reported paying for it online. In Lebanon and Vietnam, for example, more than 80 percent of adults who bought something online paid in cash on delivery.

In China, by contrast, 85 percent of adults who bought something online also paid for it online (figure 4.12). Many of them probably used popular third-party online and mobile payment platforms such as Alipay and WeChat, which were developed specifically to facilitate online payments. Indeed, Alipay's slogan is "experience fast, easy and safe online payments."

FIGURE 4.10

On average in high-income economies, two-thirds of adults use the internet to pay bills or shop online

Adults using the internet for specified purpose in the past year (%), 2017

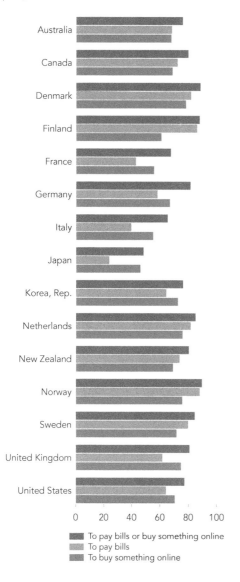

To pay bills or buy something online
To pay bills
To buy something online

Source: Global Findex database.

FIGURE 4.11

In developing economies a far smaller share of adults use the internet for paying bills or shopping online

Adults using the internet for specified purpose in the past year (%), 2017

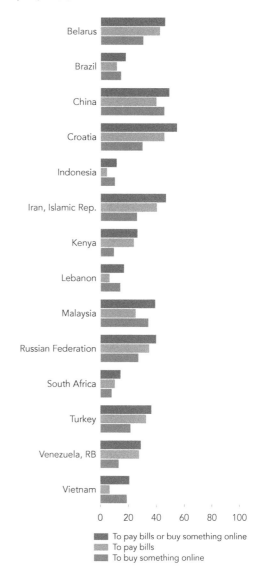

To pay bills or buy something online
To pay bills
To buy something online

Source: Global Findex database.

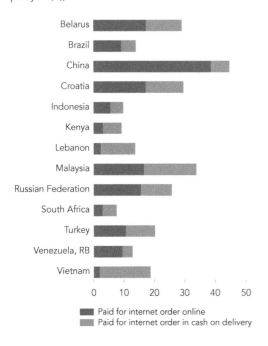

FIGURE 4.12

Online shoppers tend to pay online in China—but in cash on delivery in most other developing economies

Adults using the internet to buy something online in the past year (%), 2017

- Paid for internet order online
- Paid for internet order in cash on delivery

Source: Global Findex database.

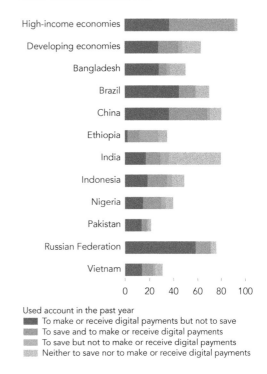

FIGURE 4.13

Most people who use their account to save also use it to make or receive digital payments

Adults with an account (%), 2017

Used account in the past year
- To make or receive digital payments but not to save
- To save and to make or receive digital payments
- To save but not to make or receive digital payments
- Neither to save nor to make or receive digital payments

Source: Global Findex database.

Use of accounts for saving

Making or receiving digital payments is one important use of an account. Saving is another. But few people reported using their account for saving but not also for making or receiving digital payments in the past year. In developing economies only 3 percent of adults did so (figure 4.13). Ethiopia is an exception to this pattern, with 15 percent of adults reporting using their account for saving but not for digital payments. Indeed, it is the only economy where this share exceeded 10 percent. In India the share was 7 percent.

Accounts that remain inactive

Globally, 13 percent of adults, or 20 percent of account owners, reported having what can be considered an inactive account, with no deposit or withdrawal —in digital form or otherwise—in the past 12 months (figure 4.14).[9] The share of

FIGURE 4.14

Globally, one in five account owners has an account that was inactive in the past year
Adults with an account (%), 2017

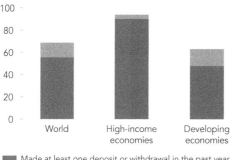

■ Made at least one deposit or withdrawal in the past year
▦ Made no deposit and no withdrawal in the past year

Source: Global Findex database.

FIGURE 4.15

In India almost half of account owners have an account that remained inactive in the past year
Adults with an account (%), 2017

■ Made at least one deposit or withdrawal in the past year
▦ Made no deposit and no withdrawal in the past year

Source: Global Findex database.

account owners with an inactive account varies across economies, but it is especially high in many South Asian economies (figure 4.15). In India the share is 48 percent—the highest in the world and about twice the average of 25 percent for developing economies. Part of the explanation might be India's Jan Dhan Yojana scheme, developed by the government to increase account ownership. Launched in August 2014, the program had brought an additional 310 million Indians into the formal banking system by March 2018, many of whom might not yet have had an opportunity to use their new account.[10] In Afghanistan, Nepal, and Sri Lanka about a third of account owners have an inactive account, while in Bangladesh 21 percent do. And Pakistan has a rate of just 13 percent, though it also has a low rate of account ownership compared with other economies in the region. In high-income economies only 4 percent of account owners have an inactive account.

In developing economies female account owners are on average 5 percentage points more likely than male account owners to have an inactive account. In India, however, this gender gap is about twice as large: while 54 percent of women with an account reported having made no deposit or withdrawal in the past year, only 43 percent of men with an account did so.

In developing economies 76 percent of adults with an inactive account have a mobile phone, including 66 percent in India. This represents an opportunity for expanding the use of accounts through digital technology—a topic explored in detail in the chapter on opportunities for expanding financial inclusion through digital technology.

Notes

1. Globally in 2017, 0.28 percent of adults reported receiving payments from self-employment into an account in the past year but not making or receiving any other digital payments. Data on payments from self-employment were not collected in 2014.
2. No comparable data on digital payments were collected in 2011.
3. Myanmar and Nepal are the only other two economies with a similarly low share of adults who reported having made or received digital payments.
4. This does not include using a card for a cash withdrawal at an ATM. No data are collected on prepaid cards not linked to an account.
5. In 2011, 69 percent of account owners in high-income economies reported having a debit card, while 57 percent of account owners in developing economies did so. No data are available on the use of cards for direct purchases for 2011.
6. "Cash Crunch: How Venezuela Inadvertently Became a Cashless Economy," *Guardian*, November 30, 2017.
7. While a credit card does not have to be linked to an account, less than 0.5 percent of adults around the world reported owning a credit card but not having an account at a financial institution.
8. Mobile money accounts are offered in only three high-income economies—Chile, Singapore, and the United Arab Emirates.
9. It is not possible to ascertain whether accounts with no deposit and no withdrawal in the past 12 months are "dormant," as they may be used for long-term saving.
10. "Pradhan Mantri Jan Dhan Yojana Progress-Report," Department of Financial Services, Indian Ministry of Finance, March 21, 2018, https://pmjdy.gov.in/account.

5 SAVING, CREDIT, AND FINANCIAL RESILIENCE

People save for future expenses—a large purchase, investments in education or a business, their needs in old age or in possible emergencies. Or, facing more immediate expenses, they may choose to borrow instead. Global Findex data show how and why people save and borrow and shed light on their financial resilience to unexpected expenses.

How and why people save

In 2017, 48 percent of adults around the world reported having saved or set aside money in the past 12 months. In high-income economies 71 percent of adults reported having saved, while in developing economies 43 percent did so.

MAP 5.1
Formal saving around the world
Adults saving at a financial institution in the past year (%), 2017

- 0–9
- 10–19
- 20–29
- 30–49
- 50–100
- No data

Source: Global Findex database.

FIGURE 5.1

Globally, more than half of adults who save choose to do so at a financial institution

Adults saving any money in the past year (%), 2017

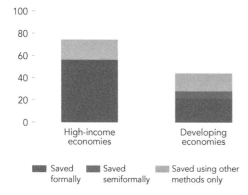

■ Saved formally ■ Saved semiformally ▨ Saved using other methods only

Source: Global Findex database.
Note: People may save in multiple ways, but categories are constructed to be mutually exclusive. *Saved formally* includes all adults who saved any money formally. *Saved semiformally* includes all adults who saved any money semiformally but not formally. Data on semiformal saving are not collected in most high-income economies.

How do people save?

People go about saving money in different ways. Globally in 2017, 27 percent of adults—or just over half of savers—reported having saved formally in the past 12 months, at a bank or another type of financial institution. Among all adults, the share who reported saving formally averaged 55 percent in high-income economies and 21 percent in developing economies (map 5.1; figure 5.1). Among savers, the share saving formally was more than three-quarters in high-income economies but just under half in developing economies.

In developing economies a common alternative to saving at a financial institution is to save semiformally, by using a savings club or a person outside the family. In 2017, 11 percent of adults—or 25 percent of savers—in developing economies reported having saved in this way, including 7 percent of adults who saved semiformally but not formally. One common type of savings club is a rotating savings and credit association. These associations generally operate by pooling weekly deposits and disbursing the entire amount to a different member each week.[1]

The options for saving go beyond doing so at a financial institution or by using a savings club or a person outside the family. In both high-income and developing economies 16 percent of adults reported saving in some other way only. This may include saving in cash at home ("under the mattress") or saving in the form of livestock, jewelry, or real estate. It may also include using investment products offered by equity and other traded markets or purchasing government securities.

How does account ownership matter for savings behavior?

Having an account is a prerequisite for saving formally.[2] And account ownership has increased steadily since the first round of Global Findex data were collected. Globally, the share of adults with an account rose from 51 percent to 69 percent between 2011 and 2017. But has formal saving also increased over time? The share of adults worldwide who reported having saved formally in the past year rose from 23 percent to 27 percent between 2011 and 2014, but then remained at that level in 2017 (figure 5.2).

With account ownership being a prerequisite for formal saving, it is no surprise that high-income economies, which have much higher account ownership on average than developing economies, also have a higher average share of adults reporting that they saved formally in the past year. As discussed in the chapter on account ownership, those who have an account also tend to be wealthier and to be participating actively in the labor force—and thus might have a greater capacity to save.

But having an account does not necessarily imply formal saving. Even among account owners there is much variation in the use of accounts for saving. Globally in 2017, 38 percent of account owners reported having saved at a financial institution in the past 12 months. But while the share who reported having done so was 58 percent in high-income economies, it was only 31 percent in developing economies (figure 5.3).

Use of accounts for saving is low even in economies where the share of adults with an account has reached about 70 percent or more. In China and Malaysia 43 percent of account owners reported having saved formally in the past year, while the share was about 30 percent in Kenya, South Africa, and Turkey—and about 20 percent in Brazil, India, and the Russian Federation. In Kenya and South Africa some 20 percent of account owners reported having saved semiformally, by using a savings club or a person outside the family. And in both high-income and developing economies almost 20 percent reported having saved exclusively in some other way.

FIGURE 5.2
More account ownership does not necessarily translate into more formal saving
Adults with an account (%)

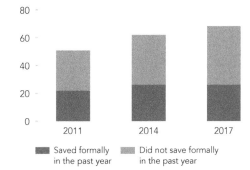

Saved formally in the past year   Did not save formally in the past year

Source: Global Findex database.

FIGURE 5.3
Account owners do not necessarily use their account to save—or even save at all
Adults with an account by savings behavior in the past year (%), 2017

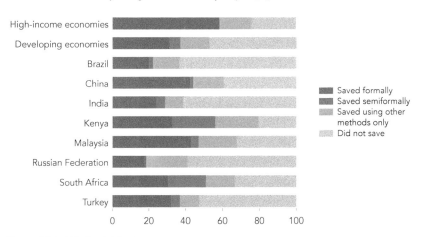

Saved formally
Saved semiformally
Saved using other methods only
Did not save

Source: Global Findex database.
Note: Account owners may save in multiple ways, but categories are constructed to be mutually exclusive. *Saved formally* includes all account owners who saved any money formally. *Saved semiformally* includes all account owners who saved any money semiformally but not formally. Data on semiformal saving are not collected in most high-income economies. In all individual economies shown, about 70 percent or more of adults have an account.

FIGURE 5.4

Almost a third of unbanked adults save
Adults by account ownership and savings behavior in
the past year (%), 2017

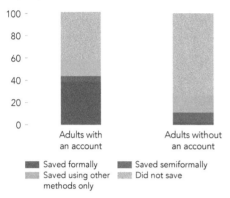

Legend:
- Saved formally
- Saved using other methods only
- Saved semiformally
- Did not save

Source: Global Findex database.
Note: People may save in multiple ways, but categories
are constructed to be mutually exclusive. *Saved
formally* includes all adults who saved any money
formally. *Saved semiformally* includes all adults who
saved any money semiformally but not formally.

Indeed, having an account does not necessarily imply that people save at all. Globally, 42 percent of account owners reported not having saved any money in the past year. In high-income economies 26 percent of account owners reported not having saved any money. And in Brazil, India, Russia, and Turkey—all economies where about 70 percent or more of adults have an account—about 60 percent reported not saving at all.

What does savings behavior look like among those without an account? Compared with those who have an account, unbanked adults might have lower income and thus lower capacity to save—and they might also have less access to convenient and affordable formal financial services. Yet 28 percent of unbanked adults around the world reported having saved in the past year (figure 5.4). Some 17 percent of unbanked adults reported having saved only in some way other than formally or semiformally, and 9 percent reported having saved semiformally—similar to the shares who reported having saved using these methods among adults with an account.[3]

How does savings behavior differ across economies and individual characteristics?

Savings behavior not only differs between high-income and developing economies; it also varies among developing economies. Consider those with some of the largest numbers of unbanked adults. Among these economies, the share of adults who reported having saved formally in the past year ranges from 35 percent in China to around 5 percent in the Democratic Republic of Congo, Côte d'Ivoire, the Arab Republic of Egypt, Pakistan, and Tanzania (figure 5.5). Indeed, China is one of five developing economies—together with Croatia, Malaysia, Namibia, and Thailand—where the share saving formally is in the 30–40 percent range (and rates of account ownership are above average).

Saving semiformally is a common method of saving especially in Sub-Saharan Africa. On average across the region, 26 percent of adults reported having saved in the past year using a savings club or a person outside the family, including 19 percent of adults who reported having saved money semiformally but not formally—and in Ethiopia, Kenya, Rwanda, and South Africa, for example, more than 20 percent reported having done so. But saving semiformally is also common in some economies outside Sub-Saharan Africa—including Indonesia and Pakistan, where about 20 percent of adults reported saving using this method.

FIGURE 5.5
Savings behavior varies widely across developing economies
Adults saving any money in the past year (%), 2017

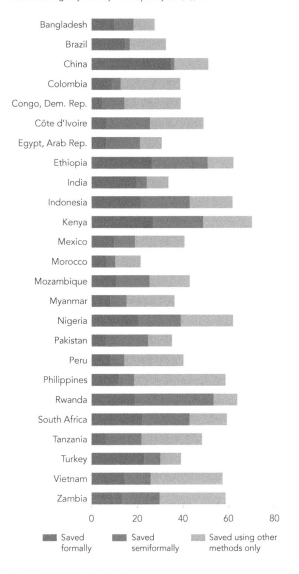

Source: Global Findex database.
Note: People may save in multiple ways, but categories are constructed to be mutually exclusive. *Saved formally* includes all adults who saved any money formally. *Saved semiformally* includes all adults who saved any money semiformally but not formally.

And in some economies the most common method of saving is in some other way than at a financial institution or by using a savings club or a person outside the family. These include Colombia, the Democratic Republic of Congo, Peru, and the Philippines, where about two-thirds of savers reported saving in some other way.

MAP 5.2
In Sub-Saharan Africa saving semiformally is much more common than saving formally
Adults saving in the past year (%), 2017

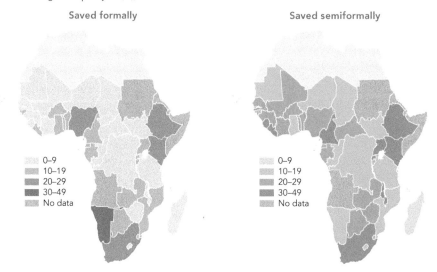

Saved formally

Saved semiformally

| 0–9 |
| 10–19 |
| 20–29 |
| 30–49 |
| No data |

Source: Global Findex database.
Note: Data are displayed only for economies in Sub-Saharan Africa.

FIGURE 5.6

In developing economies men are more likely than women to save formally
Adults saving any money in the past year (%), 2017

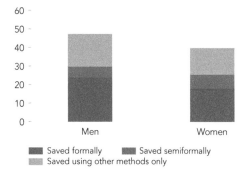

■ Saved formally   ■ Saved semiformally
■ Saved using other methods only

Source: Global Findex database.
Note: People may save in multiple ways, but categories are constructed to be mutually exclusive. *Saved formally* includes all adults who saved any money formally. *Saved semiformally* includes all adults who saved any money semiformally but not formally.

In 8 of 10 economies in Sub-Saharan Africa more adults reported having saved semiformally in the past year than reported having saved formally (map 5.2). Yet many people save both formally and semiformally. On average in the region, 9 percent of adults reported saving only formally, and 19 percent saving only semiformally. But 6 percent reported saving both formally and semiformally. This suggests that semiformal savings arrangements offer products or provide benefits—such as convenience or community building—that are not available through saving at a financial institution alone.

Savings behavior also varies by individual characteristics. In high-income economies, just as for owning an account, men and women were equally likely to report having saved at a financial institution. But in developing economies men were 6 percentage points more likely than women to report having saved formally (figure 5.6). This gender gap in formal saving is about the same as the gender gap in account ownership in developing economies. Overall, these data mean that men and women are about equally likely to use their account for saving.

FIGURE 5.7
Adults living in the poorest 40 percent of households in their economy are less likely to save formally
Adults saving any money in the past year (%), 2017

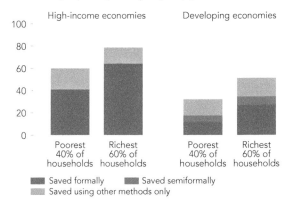

Source: Global Findex database.
Note: People may save in multiple ways, but categories are constructed to be mutually exclusive. *Saved formally* includes all adults who saved any money formally. *Saved semiformally* includes all adults who saved any money semiformally but not formally. Data on semiformal saving are not collected in most high-income economies.

Not surprisingly, adults living in the poorest 40 percent of households within economies were less likely to report having saved formally than those living in the richest 60 percent (figure 5.7). This holds in both high-income and developing economies. But while the gap in formal saving between richer and poorer adults is 15 percentage points in developing economies, it is 23 percentage points in high-income economies.

What are the main reasons for saving?

For what future expenses do people save? The 2017 Global Findex survey asked about two specific reasons for saving—for old age and to start, operate, or expand a business.[4] Globally, 21 percent of adults reported having saved in the past 12 months for old age—44 percent in high-income economies and 16 percent in developing economies. Saving to start, operate, or expand a business was reported by about 14 percent in both high-income and developing economies.

Saving for a business was especially common in many Sub-Saharan African economies. In Ethiopia, Kenya, Liberia, Nigeria, Uganda, and Zambia, for example, 29 percent or more of adults reported having done so—twice the global average. But while the majority of those saving for a business in these six economies have an account, more than half on average reported having saved only in nonformal ways, such as through a savings club or in the form of livestock, jewelry, or real estate.

FIGURE 5.8
The most common source of credit in high-income economies is formal borrowing—in developing economies, family or friends

Adults borrowing any money in the past year (%), 2017

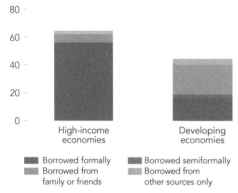

Legend:
- Borrowed formally
- Borrowed from family or friends
- Borrowed semiformally
- Borrowed from other sources only

Source: Global Findex database.
Note: People may borrow from multiple sources, but categories are constructed to be mutually exclusive. *Borrowed formally* includes all adults who borrowed any money from a financial institution or through the use of a credit card. *Borrowed semiformally* includes all adults who borrowed any money semiformally (from a savings club) but not formally. *Borrowed from family or friends* excludes adults who borrowed formally or semiformally.

How and why people borrow

Globally in 2017, 47 percent of adults reported having borrowed money in the past 12 months, including through the use of a credit card. The share of adults with new credit, formal or nonformal, averaged 64 percent across high-income economies and 44 percent across developing economies.

What are the sources of credit?

In high-income economies formal borrowing was by far the most common source of credit: almost 90 percent of borrowers reported borrowing from a financial institution or through the use of a credit card (figure 5.8; map 5.3). In developing economies family and friends were the most common source, reported by almost half of borrowers. But formal borrowing was the most common source in some developing economies, including Argentina, Brazil, China, Peru, and Turkey as well as Russia and many other economies in Europe and Central Asia (figure 5.9).

MAP 5.3
Formal borrowing around the world

Adults borrowing from a financial institution or through the use of a credit card in the past year (%), 2017

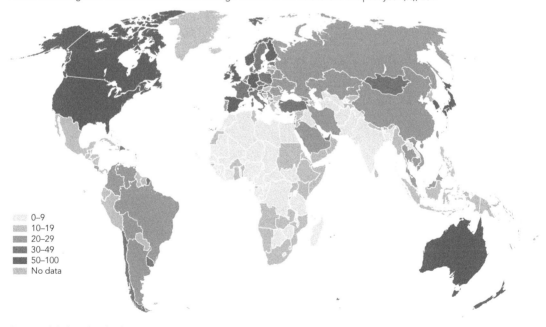

Legend:
- 0–9
- 10–19
- 20–29
- 30–49
- 50–100
- No data

Source: Global Findex database.

FIGURE 5.9

Individual developing economies show much variation in the most common source of credit

Adults borrowing any money in the past year (%), 2017

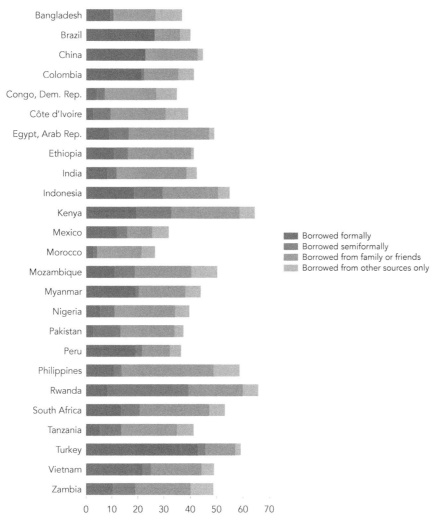

Source: Global Findex database.
Note: People may borrow from multiple sources, but categories are constructed to be mutually exclusive. *Borrowed formally* includes all adults who borrowed any money from a financial institution or through the use of a credit card. *Borrowed semiformally* includes all adults who borrowed any money semiformally (from a savings club) but not formally. *Borrowed from family or friends* excludes adults who borrowed formally or semiformally.

Borrowing semiformally, from a savings club such as a rotating savings and credit association, was reported by 3 percent of adults in developing economies. But the share was much higher in some: 31 percent in Rwanda and between 11 and 18 percent in six Sub-Saharan African economies—Cameroon, Kenya, Liberia, Malawi, Sierra Leone, and Uganda—as well as Indonesia and Pakistan. Other sources of borrowing, including private informal lenders, were reported by 4 percent of adults globally.

Globally, the share of adults reporting formal borrowing, including through the use of a credit card, remained flat between 2014 and 2017, at 23 percent.[5] This trend of credit card use remaining flat holds for both high-income and developing economies on average.

What is the role of credit cards in formal borrowing?

Credit cards are a payment instrument, but they also serve as a source of credit. Credit cards extend short-term credit whenever used, even when credit card holders pay off their balance in full each statement cycle and as a result pay no interest on that balance. The introduction of credit cards might therefore have affected the demand for and use of short-term credit. As reported in the chapter on the use of accounts, 49 percent of adults in high-income economies used a credit card in 2017. In developing economies, despite continued growth in credit card use in recent years, only 8 percent on average reported using one. But this share exceeded 15 percent in China and in some economies in Europe and Central Asia as well as Latin America and the Caribbean.

In high-income economies borrowing through the use of a credit card dominates formal borrowing. Among those who reported borrowing formally, about a third borrowed from a financial institution while two-thirds borrowed by using a credit card but did not borrow from a financial institution (figure 5.10). Among developing economies, four stand out for relatively high credit card use: Argentina, Brazil, Croatia, and Turkey, where more than 20 percent of adults reported using a credit card in the past 12 months. In these four countries, as in high-income economies, adults borrowing through the use of a credit card but not a loan from a financial institution make up about two-thirds of all those who reported borrowing formally.

FIGURE 5.10
Credit card use dominates formal borrowing in high-income economies
Adults borrowing formally in the past year (%), 2017

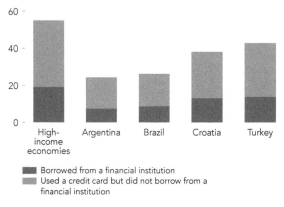

Source: Global Findex database.

For what purposes do people borrow? One common purpose is to buy land or a home, the largest financial investment that many people make in their life. In 2017, 27 percent of adults in high-income economies reported having an outstanding housing loan from a bank or another type of financial institution (map 5.4). In contrast, that share was typically less than 10 percent in developing economies. Even among high-income economies there is much variation in the share of adults with a formal housing loan. While about half of adults in the Netherlands, Norway, and Sweden reported having one, 10 percent or less did so in Chile, Greece, Latvia, and Uruguay.

The 2017 Global Findex survey asked whether people had borrowed money in the past 12 months for health or medical purposes or to start, operate, or expand a business.[6] This could have been money borrowed from any source, including a financial institution, a savings club, and family or friends.

In developing economies 11 percent of adults reported having borrowed in the past year for health or medical purposes. Among this group, 79 percent reported having borrowed only from family or friends or from other nonformal sources. Borrowing to start, operate, or expand a business was reported by 7 percent of adults in developing economies overall. On average, about half of them reported

MAP 5.4
Formal housing finance outstanding around the world
Adults with an outstanding loan from a financial institution to purchase a home or land (%), 2017

0–9
10–19
20–29
30–100
No data

Source: Global Findex database.

having borrowed from a financial institution and half from family or friends or other nonformal sources. In high-income economies less than 5 percent of adults reported having borrowed for health or medical purposes or to start, operate, or expand a business.

The survey also asked about both saving and borrowing to start, operate, or expand a business. Saving and borrowing are two basic ways to finance investments in business. In developing economies 18 percent of adults reported having either saved or borrowed for a business. Most of them saved: 11 percent of adults had only saved, 3 percent had saved and borrowed, and 4 percent had only borrowed. It is notable that twice as many reported having saved for a business as reported having borrowed for one—though that may in part reflect a pattern in which people may save long before starting a business but borrow only once the business is about to start operation. Nevertheless, this highlights the need for both savings and credit products for business owners.

Financial resilience

Financial inclusion is not an end in itself but a means to an end—when people have a safe place to save money as well as access to credit when needed, they are better able to manage financial risk. To better understand how financially resilient people around the world are to unexpected expenses, the 2017 Global Findex survey asked respondents whether or not it would be possible to come up with an amount equal to 1/20 of gross national income (GNI) per capita in local currency within the next month. It also asked what their main source of funding would be.

Globally, 54 percent of adults reported that it would be possible to come up with this amount. In high-income economies 73 percent said that it would be possible. In developing economies a smaller share did so, 50 percent. But the ability to come up with emergency funds is not just a function of the income level in an economy. In Ethiopia, a low-income economy, 57 percent of adults said that it would be possible to come up with the emergency funds, the same share as in China, an upper-middle-income economy. And just under half of adults reported that it would be possible in both Brazil, an upper-middle-income economy, and India, a lower-middle-income one. It is also possible that cultural differences across economies influence the type of emergency people are imagining or whether people are inclined to say that it is possible to come up with emergency funds.

In high-income economies women were about as likely as men to say that it would be possible to come up with the money. But in developing economies women were 11 percentage points less likely than men to say this. Not surprisingly, there were also differences by income level: adults living in the poorest 40 percent of households within economies were on average 27 percentage points less likely to say they could come up with the funds than those living in the richest 60 percent. This holds in both high-income and developing economies.

What are the sources of emergency funds?

Among those saying that it would be possible to come up with the funds, what would be their main source of funding? Globally, savings, money from working, and family or friends were each named by about a third of these respondents—or just under 20 percent of all adults. But while in high-income economies the majority of those able to come up with the emergency funds (or 43 percent of all adults) cited savings as their main source, in developing economies two-thirds (or 34 percent of all adults) cited either money from working or family and friends as their main source (figure 5.11). Borrowing from a bank, an employer, or a private lender was cited as the main source of emergency funds by 7 percent of adults in high-income economies, but by only a negligible share in developing economies. Other sources of funds were cited by less than 3 percent of adults globally.

Among those who cited savings as their main source of funding, three-quarters reported having saved at a financial institution in high-income economies but only half did so in developing economies. Does it matter how people save for a potential emergency? Savings in any form that can be readily accessed can help people handle emergencies. But saving in nonformal ways—such as through a savings club or in the form of livestock, jewelry, or real estate—may mean that the savings will not be readily accessible in an emergency. The savings club might have spent the money, and selling livestock, jewelry, or real estate quickly or without a loss might not be possible. And while saving cash at home may keep it readily accessible, saving money at a bank or another type of financial institution offers potential advantages. One is safety from theft. Another is that formal saving can curb impulse spending and therefore encourage better cash management, ensuring that money is available in an emergency.

Relying on money from working or family and friends as the main source of emergency funds is a pattern replicated in many developing economies. But these two sources are not necessarily cited in equal proportion in every economy. Money from working was most commonly cited as the main source of funds in China, Indonesia, and Tanzania—and family or friends as the main source in Brazil, Egypt, and India (figure 5.12). In Ethiopia the two sources were equally likely to be cited by those able to come up with emergency funds. In Kenya three sources—money from working, family or friends, and savings—were all equally likely to be cited. Pakistan is among the few developing economies where savings was most commonly cited as the main source of funds—reported by 20 percent of adults. But among this group, only about 1 in 10 reported having saved at a financial institution in the past year, while the rest saved in nonformal ways.

FIGURE 5.11

People in high-income economies are more likely to be able to raise emergency funds—and to do so through savings
Adults able to raise emergency funds (%), 2017

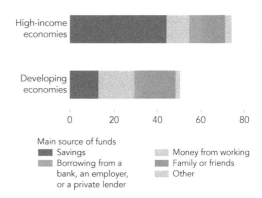

Main source of funds
- Savings
- Borrowing from a bank, an employer, or a private lender
- Money from working
- Family or friends
- Other

Source: Global Findex database.
Note: Other includes all respondents who chose "selling assets," "other sources," "don't know," or "refuse" as their response for main source of emergency funds.

FIGURE 5.12

People in different developing economies may turn to different sources for emergency funds

Adults able to raise emergency funds (%), 2017

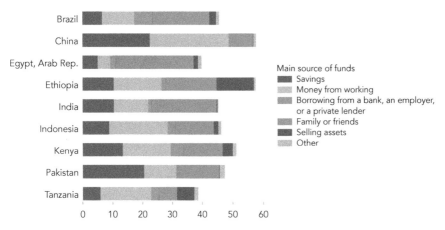

Source: Global Findex database.
Note: Other includes all respondents who chose "other sources," "don't know," or "refuse" as their response for main source of emergency funds.

FIGURE 5.13

For adults active in the labor force in developing economies, money from working is the main source of emergency funds

Adults able to raise emergency funds (%), 2017

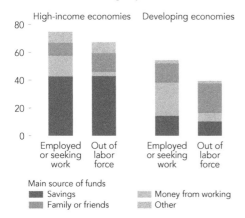

Sources: Global Findex database; Gallup World Poll 2017.
Note: Other includes all respondents who chose "borrowing from a bank, an employer, or a private lender," "selling assets," "other sources," "don't know," or "refuse" as their response for main source of emergency funds.

Not surprisingly, money from working was much more likely to be reported as the main source of emergency funds by adults active in the labor force. These respondents were about four times as likely to cite this source in both high-income and developing economies (figure 5.13). Relying on money from working could be interpreted as working more—by putting in more hours or seeking additional work—or receiving a salary advance from an employer. But people might also interpret money from working as the regular salary they receive for their labor. In this case these funds could also be considered savings, since any share of salary that is not spent is technically savings. But respondents did not consider money from working to be savings, which was a separate response option for the main source of emergency funds.

Adults active in the labor force were also more likely to report that it would be possible to come up with emergency funds. In high-income economies on average they were about 7 percentage points more likely to do so than adults out of the labor force—and in developing economies on average, about 15 percentage points more likely to do so. And for those active in the labor force in developing economies who said that it would be possible to come up with emergency funds, money from working was by far the most common source—cited by 24 percent of this group (see figure 5.13).

What is the exposure to financial risk in agriculture?

The ability to manage financial risk is especially important for people earning their living in agriculture by growing crops or raising livestock, because of their exposure to weather and disease shocks. A new survey module on financial risk management in agriculture, used for adults living in households engaged in growing crops or raising livestock in selected developing economies, sheds new light on the extent of this exposure.[7] Among adults in the surveyed economies, about 4 in 10 in East Asia and the Pacific, 4 in 10 in South Asia, and 5 in 10 in Sub-Saharan Africa reported living in a household where growing crops or raising livestock is a main source of household income. About half these adults reported that their household had experienced a bad harvest or significant livestock loss in the past five years. And most of these households bear the entire financial risk of such a loss, receiving no compensation through either an insurance payout or government assistance.

This overall pattern is replicated across economies. Consider Uganda, representative of the exposure to financial risk in agriculture for adults in low- and lower-middle-income economies in Sub-Saharan Africa: Just over half of adults in that country reported growing crops or raising livestock as a main source of their household's income, while a quarter of adults reported that their household had experienced a bad harvest or significant livestock loss in the past five years. And only 10 percent reported having received compensation for such a loss (figure 5.14).

FIGURE 5.14

Among agricultural households experiencing a bad harvest or significant loss of livestock in Sub-Saharan Africa, most bear all the financial risk themselves

Adults living in a household where growing crops or raising livestock is a main source of household income (%), 2017

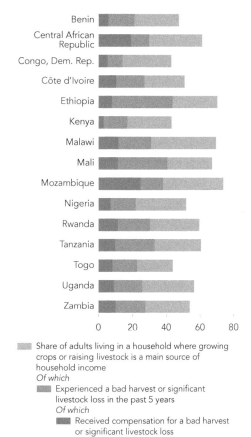

Share of adults living in a household where growing crops or raising livestock is a main source of household income
Of which
　　Experienced a bad harvest or significant livestock loss in the past 5 years
　　Of which
　　　　Received compensation for a bad harvest or significant livestock loss

Source: Global Findex database.
Note: The total length of each bar represents the share of adults living in a household where growing crops or raising livestock is a main source of household income.

Notes

1. Although savings clubs often require a commitment to regular periodic saving outside the home, they are referred to in this report as a semiformal savings option because they may not ensure that money is safe from theft or loss and because they do not allow those who use them to make payments from their account or to build a personal savings history.
2. Globally, 3 percent of unbanked adults reported having saved formally.
3. The numbers for savings behavior by adults with and without an account in developing economies are the same as the global numbers, except that the share of adults with an account who reported saving formally is 31 percent in developing economies as compared with 38 percent globally.
4. Saving for a business also includes saving to start, operate, or expand a farm.
5. The 2011 Global Findex survey asked only about ownership of a credit card (not the use of one), so no comparable measure can be constructed for 2011. The share of adults reporting formal borrowing excluding through the use of a credit card has remained flat at 11 percent.
6. Borrowing for a business also includes borrowing to start, operate, or expand a farm.
7. Additional work is under way on a comprehensive analysis of the agricultural financial risk management module.

SPOTLIGHT

ACCESS TO MOBILE PHONES AND THE INTERNET AROUND THE WORLD

Mobile phones and the internet have created new opportunities for providing financial services. Relatively simple, text-based mobile phones allow the use of mobile money accounts, for example, and smartphone technology provides a convenient means for people to make transactions from their financial institution account. But people's ability to use digital financial services like these depends on their having access to the necessary technology. How many people around the world own a mobile phone and have access to the internet?

According to 2017 Gallup World Poll data, 93 percent of adults in high-income economies have their own mobile phone, while 79 percent do in developing economies (map S.1). In India 69 percent of adults have a mobile phone, as do 85 percent in Brazil and 93 percent in China.

Women are less likely than men to have a mobile phone. In developing economies 84 percent of men and 74 percent of women own a mobile phone, reflecting a gender gap of 10 percentage points. The gap is bigger in some economies. In Pakistan, for example, men are more than twice as likely as women to have a mobile phone. Yet several developing economies have no appreciable gender gap, including Brazil, China, Colombia, Indonesia, and Turkey.

Not surprisingly, there is also a gap in mobile phone ownership between richer and poorer adults. Globally, 85 percent of adults living in the richest 60 percent of households within economies have a mobile phone, compared with 76 percent of those living in the poorest 40 percent. Bigger gaps are found in the developing world, particularly Sub-Saharan Africa. Ethiopia, Mozambique, Tanzania, and Zambia are among the economies where the gap is 20 percentage points or more. In Côte d'Ivoire, however, the share of poorer adults who have a mobile phone, at 75 percent, is roughly the same as the share of wealthier adults who have one.

Having access to the internet as well as a mobile phone brings a wider range of financial services within reach. In high-income economies 82 percent of adults have both a mobile phone and access to the internet, indicating a likelihood that they have access to app-based mobile phone or online payments. In developing economies only 40 percent of adults—or about half of mobile phone owners—have access to both technologies.

Mobile phone ownership around the world
Adults with a mobile phone (%), 2017

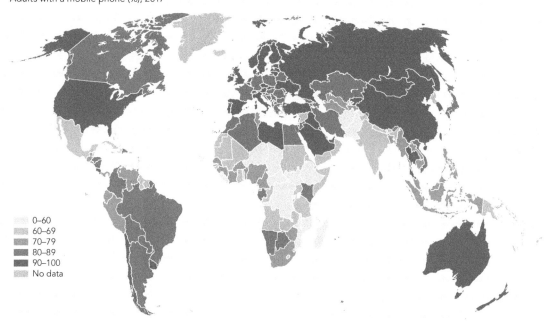

0–60
60–69
70–79
80–89
90–100
No data

Source: Gallup World Poll 2017.

In developing economies, while 43 percent of men have both a mobile phone and access to the internet, 37 percent of women do—a gender gap of 6 percentage points. Men are twice as likely as women to have access to both these technologies in some economies, including Bangladesh, Ethiopia, and India. But men and women have equal access in China, Colombia, and South Africa.

Wealthier adults are more likely than their poorer counterparts to have access to both a mobile phone and the internet. In the developing world 48 percent of adults in the richest 60 percent of households within economies have these technologies, while 28 percent of those in the poorest 40 percent do—a gap of 20 percentage points. In Kenya the gap is nearly twice as large, at 39 percentage points; in Colombia it is 29 percentage points.

6 OPPORTUNITIES FOR EXPANDING FINANCIAL INCLUSION THROUGH DIGITAL TECHNOLOGY

Global Findex data reveal many opportunities to increase account ownership among the 1.7 billion adults who remain unbanked. The data also point to ways to leverage new products and technologies to boost the use of accounts among those who already have one. This chapter outlines opportunities focused on moving into accounts the transactions that people are already making in cash.

Shifting payments from cash into accounts can have benefits beyond expanding account ownership and increasing account use. Research suggests that digitizing payments can improve their efficiency by increasing the speed of payments and reducing the cost of disbursing and receiving them.[1] It can also enhance the security of payments and thus lower the incidence of associated crime.[2] And disbursing payments through digital channels rather than cash has been shown to increase transparency and reduce corruption.[3] Moreover, by providing an important first entry point into the formal financial system, shifting to digital payments can lead to substantial increases in saving as well as the substitution of formal for informal saving.[4]

For businesses and governments alike, however, the challenge is to ensure that digital payments are indeed better than the cash-based alternatives—safer, more affordable, and more transparent.

The landscape for digital payments

Mobile phones and the internet have given rise to a new generation of financial services. Using these services does not necessarily require sophisticated devices. In Sub-Saharan Africa relatively simple, text-based mobile phones have powered the spread of mobile money accounts. Similar services are available in other parts of the developing world. And smartphone technology is increasingly being used to make transactions through financial institution accounts in some developing economies.

But mobile phones and the internet can drive financial inclusion only if they are underpinned by the necessary infrastructure. Physical infrastructure—such as reliable electricity and mobile networks—is key. People will be less inclined to use digital payments if network outages or other technical problems undermine their dependability. Financial infrastructure is also needed. This includes both an adequate payments system and a physical network to deliver payments to all corners of an economy—both urban and rural. While financial institutions might not find it cost-effective to open a brick-and-mortar branch in every place that has a large unbanked population, they can use agent banking—forming partnerships with post offices or retail shops to offer basic financial services to customers. People using digital payments need to be able to deposit and withdraw cash safely, reliably, and conveniently at cash-in and cash-out points, whether these take the form of a bank agent, a mobile money agent, or an automated teller machine (ATM).[5] Ideally, people receiving digital payments would keep their funds in digital form and make purchases and pay bills electronically. But in many places digital payments are not yet widely accepted for everyday purchases at local retail stores and markets, especially in developing economies. So most people need to be able to cash out at least some of the money they receive through digital payments. Indeed, a reliable cash-out experience is key to the success of digital payments.[6]

Technology and infrastructure are only part of the picture. To ensure that people benefit from digital financial services, governments need to ensure that appropriate regulations and consumer protection safeguards are in place. And regardless of the technology used, financial services need to be tailored to the needs of disadvantaged groups such as women, poor people, and first-time users, who may have low literacy and numeracy skills. Also important is to look at who has access to the digital technology needed to use the services—and who does not.

Creating an enabling environment

As this chapter shows, digitizing payments of wages and government benefits has the potential to increase both the ownership and use of accounts. Yet efforts to digitize such payments have suffered from shortcomings. A common complaint among those receiving government transfers as digital payments is that the payment products are difficult to use. Recipients have reported long lines at bank agents and said that they struggle to get help when they have a question or a problem with their payments. Others have reported being targeted for fraud.[7]

Putting in place consumer protection rules is critical to safeguard people from fraud and abuse.[8] Such protections are especially important for women and low-income people, who are most likely to be financially inexperienced. This underscores the importance of targeted financial literacy and capability training, which can have a positive impact in such areas as increasing saving and promoting financial skills like record keeping.[9] Also needed are regulations to facilitate financial inclusion, such as by introducing tiered documentation requirements, requiring banks to offer basic or low-fee accounts, and embracing opportunities to use new technologies to expand access to formal financial services.[10]

Where lack of trust in financial institutions is an important barrier to account ownership, quality product design and strong consumer protection standards could potentially help increase financial inclusion. Distrust has many causes, including government seizures of banks, discrimination against certain population groups, and past episodes of hyperinflation and bank failures. Individual financial service providers might not be able to address systemic causes of mistrust. But they can shore up trust in their own products by treating people fairly and providing quick, convenient, and effective redress in response to consumer concerns. Such efforts are critical in ensuring that newly banked adults benefit from financial inclusion.

Digital technology–based biometric identification cards provide another way of lowering barriers to account ownership. In India, where 90 percent of unbanked adults reported having proof of identity issued by the national government, recent research suggests that government-provided biometric identification cards were among the factors enabling a rapid decline in the number of adults without an account.[11] Research in Malawi suggests that biometric identification has increased loan repayment rates among borrowers most at risk of default.[12]

Splicing Global Findex data with new data from the World Bank Identification for Development (ID4D) project reveals fresh insights into the relationship between account ownership and access to documentation. In developing economies 85 percent of adults without an account at a financial institution have government-issued identification.[13] Yet in Sub-Saharan Africa, where those without a financial institution account were especially likely to cite documentation requirements as a barrier, only 56 percent of adults reported having government-issued identification.

Improving access to the government-issued identification required by know-your-customer (KYC) regulations often is not enough to increase account ownership, however, even where many people without a financial institution account cite documentation requirements as a barrier to opening one. One reason is that national identification does not always satisfy the documentation requirements. People often need to show local identification as well—such as a utility bill with a home address—and this can be hard to come by.

Leveraging digital technology among the unbanked

In many high-income economies debit and credit cards used at point-of-sale (POS) terminals dominate the digital payments landscape. In most developing economies, by contrast, few people have such cards. But many have a mobile phone, which could allow these economies to leapfrog directly to mobile payments.

Simply having a mobile phone can potentially allow access to mobile money accounts and other text- or app-based financial accounts. Having access to the internet as well expands the possibilities. Indeed, Global Findex data suggest that mobile phones and the internet could go a long way toward helping to overcome some of the barriers that unbanked adults say prevent them from accessing financial services. For example, digital financial services might shrink the distance between financial institutions and their customers. And by lowering the cost of providing financial services, digital technology might be helpful for

MAP 6.1
Two-thirds of unbanked adults have a mobile phone
Adults without an account owning a mobile phone, 2017

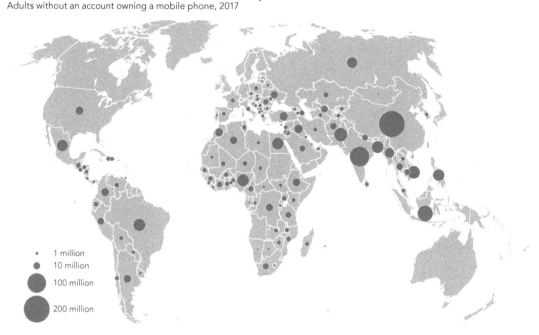

Sources: Global Findex database; Gallup World Poll 2017.
Note: Data are not displayed for economies where the share of adults without an account is 5 percent or less.

FIGURE 6.1

Mobile phone ownership among the unbanked varies across economies but tends to be high
Adults without an account (%), 2017

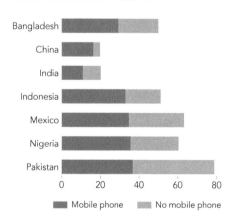

Sources: Global Findex database; Gallup World Poll 2017.

those citing high costs as a reason for not having an account at a financial institution.

Global Findex data show that mobile phone ownership is widespread among the unbanked. Globally, about 1.1 billion unbanked adults—about two-thirds of all those without an account—have a mobile phone (map 6.1).

But mobile phone ownership in this group varies among economies. Consider the seven economies that are home to nearly half the world's unbanked adults (figure 6.1). Except in Pakistan, more than half of unbanked adults have a mobile phone, and in China the share is as high as 82 percent.

Unbanked women are less likely than their male counterparts to own a mobile phone. Globally, 72 percent of unbanked men have a mobile phone, compared with 62 percent of unbanked women—a gender gap of 10 percentage points. But this gender gap differs among developing economies. In Indonesia and South Africa unbanked women are just as likely as unbanked men to have a mobile phone. Yet large gender gaps are found in Nigeria and Pakistan.

Among the unbanked in Sub-Saharan Africa, 54 percent of men have a mobile phone while 43 percent of women do—a gender gap of 11 percentage points. Yet in several economies in the region, including Mozambique and Senegal, unbanked women are about as likely as their male counterparts to own a mobile phone (figure 6.2). And in some economies, such as Botswana and Zimbabwe, unbanked women are more likely than unbanked men to have a mobile phone.

Notably, mobile phone ownership is also high among adults without a financial institution account who cited distance as a barrier: globally, 64 percent reported owning a mobile phone. The share is even higher in some economies with remote areas or remote islands where digital financial services could be especially effective. In Indonesia, for example, where 33 percent of adults without a financial institution account cited distance as a barrier, 69 percent of this group reported having a mobile phone. And in the Philippines, among the 41 percent citing distance as a barrier, 71 percent reported owning a mobile phone.

Not surprisingly, a smaller share of unbanked adults have both a mobile phone and access to the internet in some form—whether through a smartphone, a home computer, an internet café, or some other method. Globally, this share is about 25 percent. But there are big differences among major developing economies (figure 6.3). In Brazil nearly 60 percent of unbanked adults have access to both technologies. In South Africa about 33 percent do, in China 25 percent do, and in Indonesia almost 20 percent do. The share drops to about 10 percent in Bangladesh, Nigeria, and Pakistan.

FIGURE 6.2

In Sub-Saharan Africa mobile phone ownership offers large opportunities among the unbanked
Adults without an account (%), 2017

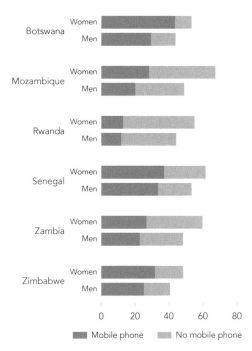

Sources: Global Findex database; Gallup World Poll 2017.

FIGURE 6.3

The unbanked are relatively unlikely to have both a mobile phone and access to the internet
Adults without an account (%), 2017

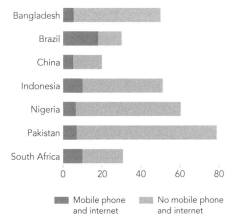

Sources: Global Findex database; Gallup World Poll 2017.

Opportunities for expanding account ownership among the unbanked

Millions of unbanked adults around the world still receive regular payments in cash—for wages, from the government, for the sale of agricultural products. Digitizing such payments is a proven way to increase account ownership. Globally, 9 percent of adults—or 13 percent of account owners—opened their first account specifically to receive private sector wages, government payments, or payments for the sale of agricultural products. The share is higher in many economies (figure 6.4). In the Islamic Republic of Iran, Malaysia, and Zambia nearly 20 percent of account owners opened their first account to receive such digital payments. The same is true for about 25 percent of account owners in Argentina, Peru, the Russian Federation, and Turkey—and for about 40 percent in the Arab Republic of Egypt and Kazakhstan.

There is room to build on this progress. This section outlines opportunities to increase account ownership by moving regular cash payments into accounts.

Digitizing payments from government to people

Governments make several types of payments to people—paying wages to public sector employees, distributing public sector pensions, and providing government transfers to those needing social benefits. Globally, about 100 million unbanked adults receive such payments in cash (map 6.2). These include 60 million women as well as 55 million adults in the poorest 40 percent of households within economies. These numbers suggest the potential for increasing account ownership by moving these payments into accounts.

Indeed, Global Findex data show that digitizing government payments has already had an effect in increasing account ownership. Among adults around the world who already have an account, roughly 80 million opened their first account to collect public

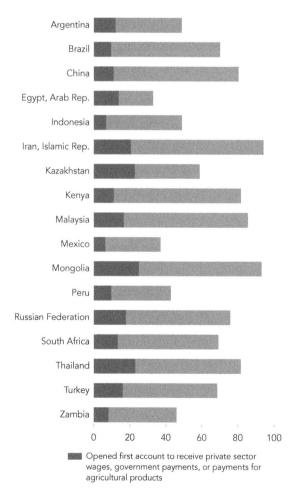

FIGURE 6.4

Millions of adults opened their first account to receive digital payments
Adults with an account (%), 2017

Legend: Opened first account to receive private sector wages, government payments, or payments for agricultural products

Source: Global Findex database.

MAP 6.2
About 100 million unbanked adults receive government payments in cash
Adults without an account receiving government payments in the past year in cash only, 2017

Source: Global Findex database.
Note: Data are not displayed for economies where the share of adults without an account is 5 percent or less or the share receiving government payments is 10 percent or less.

sector wage payments, including 35 million women. About 140 million account owners opened their first account to receive government transfers—including 80 million women as well as nearly 75 million adults in the poorest 40 percent of households. And about 120 million adults opened their first account to receive a public sector pension.[14]

Digital payments of public sector wages alone have spurred big increases in account ownership in some developing economies. In Uzbekistan 17 percent of adults with an account opened their first account to collect public sector wages; in Jordan 10 percent did so.

Digital payments of government transfers have had a similar impact. Among adults in Argentina who have an account, about 11 percent opened their first account to receive government transfers. In Thailand 14 percent did so.

Women and poorer adults may benefit disproportionately when governments digitize transfer payments. Among women with an account in Brazil, about 10 percent got their first account to receive government transfers. In Argentina nearly a quarter of account owners in the poorest 40 percent of households opened their first account for the same reason—and in Thailand 17 percent did so.

FIGURE 6.5

Digitizing government payments to people could reduce the number of unbanked

Adults without an account (%), 2017

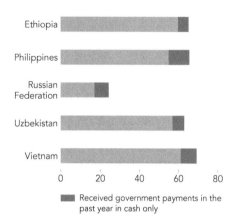

Received government payments in the
past year in cash only

Source: Global Findex database.

Digital payments of public sector pensions have also increased account ownership. In Egypt about 14 percent of account owners opened their first account to receive such payments, as did roughly 10 percent in Russia and Turkey.

Important opportunities remain to increase account ownership by moving government payments into accounts. In Vietnam 12 percent of unbanked adults receive such payments in cash; the share is similar in Ethiopia and Uzbekistan and twice as high in Russia (figure 6.5). In the Philippines digitizing government payments could reduce the share of unbanked adults by up to 16 percent and the share of unbanked women by up to 20 percent.

Governments in East Asia and the Pacific could potentially bring millions of unbanked adults into the formal financial system by distributing transfers through digital payments rather than in cash. In Vietnam nearly 4 million unbanked adults receive government transfers in cash—and in Indonesia and the Philippines about 6 million do. In Europe and Central Asia digitizing public sector pension payments could have a big impact. In Russia and Ukraine about a quarter of unbanked adults receive such payments in cash. In Romania about a third do.

Many unbanked adults receiving government payments in cash—whether government transfers or public sector wages or pensions—have the basic technology needed to receive these payments in digital form. Of the 60 million unbanked adults worldwide who receive government transfers in cash, two-thirds have a mobile phone. Among the 4 million in Vietnam, 72 percent have a mobile phone. And among the 6 million in the Philippines, 58 percent do.

Digitizing payments from businesses to people

Just as for governments, Global Findex data show that businesses could boost account ownership by paying their unbanked employees through accounts rather than in cash. Globally, 13 percent of unbanked adults—about 230 million people—receive private sector wage payments in cash, including 80 million women as well as 100 million adults in the poorest 40 percent of households within economies (map 6.3). And 78 percent of these wage earners have a mobile phone.

Moving payments of private sector wages into accounts has already proved to be effective in increasing account ownership. Globally, about 200 million adults

MAP 6.3

About 230 million unbanked adults in private sector jobs are paid in cash

Adults without an account receiving private sector wages in the past year in cash only, 2017

- · 100,000
- • 1 million
- ● 10 million

Source: Global Findex database.
Note: Data are not displayed for economies where the share of adults without an account is 5 percent or less or where the share receiving private sector wage payments is 10 percent or less.

opened their first account to collect wage payments from a private sector employer. These include 85 million women as well as 50 million adults in the poorest 40 percent of households.

Digitizing private sector wage payments could reduce the number of unbanked adults by up to a fifth in Argentina, Colombia, and Egypt and by up to almost a third in Indonesia and the Philippines. In Indonesia alone, that would mean expanding account ownership to up to 25 million unbanked adults. Large shares of these wage earners already have a mobile phone that could help facilitate electronic wage payments (figure 6.6). In Nepal, among the 20 percent of unbanked adults who receive private sector wage payments in cash, 70 percent have a mobile phone. In some developing economies mobile phone ownership among this group is considerably higher—about 90 percent in Argentina, Egypt, and Vietnam.

FIGURE 6.6

Most unbanked adults receiving private sector wages in cash have a mobile phone

Adults without an account (%), 2017

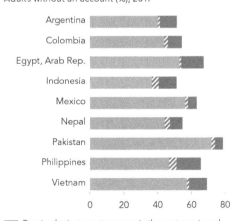

■ Received private sector wages in the past year in cash only and had a mobile phone
▨ Received private sector wages in the past year in cash only and did not have a mobile phone

Sources: Global Findex database; Gallup World Poll 2017.

Another opportunity to increase account ownership is in digitizing payments for the sale of agricultural products. About 235 million unbanked adults in developing economies receive such payments in cash, among them 110 million women as well as 125 million adults in the poorest 40 percent of households (map 6.4).

But many other people have received agricultural payments into an account. In developing economies about 40 million adults with an account opened their first one to receive payments for the sale of agricultural products.

Yet there is room to do much more. Digitizing agricultural payments could cut the number of unbanked adults by up to a quarter or more in Mozambique, Nigeria, and Vietnam; by up to roughly a third in Burkina Faso and Sierra Leone; and by up to half or more in Ethiopia (figure 6.7).

Making agricultural payments through mobile phones could be especially helpful for unbanked farmers living in remote rural areas—many of whom have access to a phone. Among unbanked adults receiving agricultural payments in cash, 59 percent have a mobile phone. In Ethiopia and Sierra Leone only about 33 percent do. But the share is nearly twice as large in Côte d'Ivoire and Nigeria.

MAP 6.4

About 235 million unbanked adults receive agricultural payments in cash
Adults without an account receiving payments for agricultural products in the past year in cash only, 2017

1 million
10 million
100 million

Source: Global Findex database.
Note: Data are not displayed for economies where the share of adults without an account is 5 percent or less or where the share receiving payments for agricultural products is 10 percent or less.

Digitizing domestic remittances and formalizing saving

The common practice of sending money to friends or relatives in another part of the country also offers opportunities for increasing account ownership. In developing economies 260 million unbanked adults—16 percent of all those without an account—send or receive domestic remittances in cash or using an over-the-counter (OTC) service such as Western Union (map 6.5). That number includes about 140 million unbanked women. Domestic remittances are most common in Sub-Saharan Africa, where they are sent or received in cash or using an OTC service by roughly a quarter of unbanked adults —about 90 million in all.

Moving domestic remittances into accounts could be an especially effective way to increase account ownership in several economies (figure 6.8). In Nigeria 37 percent of unbanked adults use domestic remittances; similar shares do so in Côte d'Ivoire, the Philippines, and South Africa.

The most common method for sending or receiving domestic remittances varies across economies. In the Philippines and South Africa unbanked adults are more likely to use an OTC

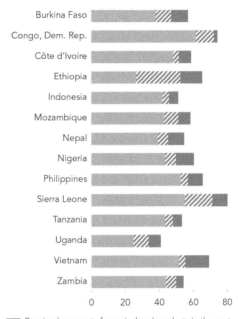

FIGURE 6.7

Digitizing agricultural payments could reduce the number of unbanked adults
Adults without an account (%), 2017

■ Received payments for agricultural products in the past year in cash only and had a mobile phone
▨ Received payments for agricultural products in the past year in cash only and did not have a mobile phone

Sources: Global Findex database; Gallup World Poll 2017.

service. But they are more likely to use cash in Nigeria as well as in Egypt and most other economies in the Middle East and North Africa. Compared with those who use cash for remittances, people who use OTC services represent a potentially easier opportunity to increase account ownership. Because these people are already comfortable with digital payments, they might find it easier to make the transition to using an account—while those who have never made digital payments might be skeptical about entrusting their money to a financial service provider. But the challenge will be to design a product that can compete with an OTC transaction on costs: one reason that people rely on an OTC service rather than an account to send domestic remittances electronically is that using an OTC service can be less expensive.[15]

Unbanked adults also use varied methods of saving. Among those who save semiformally, some entrust their money to a person outside the family. Many, particularly in Sub-Saharan Africa, rely on a savings club. One example is a rotating savings and credit association, which typically operates by pooling members' weekly deposits and disbursing the entire amount to a different member each week. Many people who choose to save semiformally may be drawn to the social

MAP 6.5

About 260 million unbanked adults use cash or an OTC service for domestic remittances

Adults without an account sending or receiving domestic remittances in the past year in cash or using an OTC service only, 2017

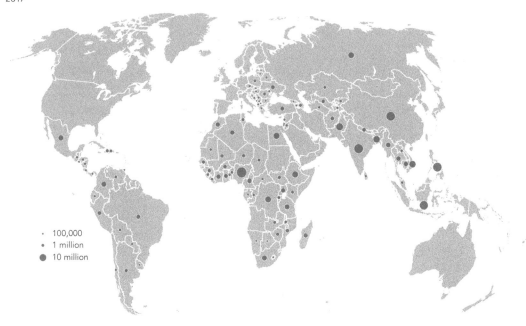

· 100,000
· 1 million
● 10 million

Source: Global Findex database.
Note: Data are not displayed for economies where the share of adults without an account is 5 percent or less or where the share sending or receiving domestic remittances is 10 percent or less.

FIGURE 6.8

Digitizing domestic remittances could have a big effect in some economies

Adults without an account (%), 2017

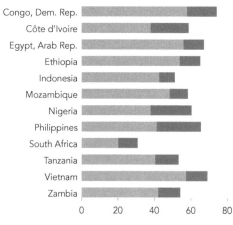

■ Sent or received domestic remittances in the past year in cash or using an OTC service only

Source: Global Findex database.

aspect of savings clubs. But using an account might be an attractive option if financial institutions offered free or low-cost interest-bearing savings products requiring little or no minimum balance. And moving semiformal saving into accounts represents an important opportunity to increase financial inclusion.

In developing economies about 150 million unbanked adults—nearly 1 in 10—save semiformally (map 6.6). In Sub-Saharan Africa alone,

MAP 6.6
Nearly 1 in 10 unbanked adults saves using semiformal methods
Adults without an account saving semiformally in the past year, 2017

Source: Global Findex database.
Note: Data are not displayed for economies where the share of adults without an account is 5 percent or less or where the share saving semiformally is 10 percent or less. Data on semiformal saving are not collected in most high-income economies.

up to 65 million unbanked adults save semi-formally, including 35 million women. Moving semiformal saving into accounts could reduce the number of unbanked adults by up to 23 per-cent in Nigeria and by up to 32 percent in Ethio-pia (figure 6.9). Semiformal savings methods are also widely used in some economies outside Sub-Saharan Africa—including by almost a fifth of unbanked adults in Pakistan and nearly a quarter of those in Indonesia.

FIGURE 6.9
Millions of unbanked adults in Sub-Saharan Africa save using semiformal methods
Adults without an account (%), 2017

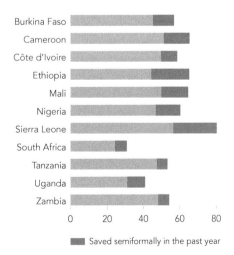

Source: Global Findex database.

Opportunities for increasing the use of accounts among the banked

Although financial inclusion starts with having an account, its benefits come from actively using that account—for saving, for managing risk, for making or receiving payments. Just as there are opportunities to increase account ownership, so are there opportunities to help people who already have an account make better use of it.

Most people do take advantage of their accounts: globally, only 20 percent of adults with an account reported that it was inactive, with no deposit or withdrawal in the past year. Yet Global Findex data suggest several ways to further increase the use of accounts among all account owners. This is not simply a matter of account owners choosing to use accounts rather than cash. Financial service providers need to offer safe, affordable, and convenient products that make using accounts more appealing than using cash.

How governments choose to make payments to people also matters. Many governments already use digital payment channels to pay public sector employees and distribute social benefits and public sector pensions. But in some economies opportunities remain to strengthen governments' use of digital payments. Globally, 2 percent of account owners—90 million adults who have an account —receive government transfers, public sector pensions, or public sector wages in cash. The share is as high as 12 percent in Ethiopia and 14 percent in the Philippines.

FIGURE 6.10

Millions of account owners receive private sector wages in cash
Adults with an account (%), 2017

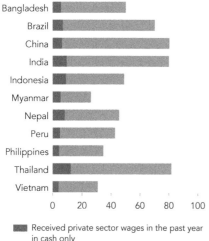

■ Received private sector wages in the past year in cash only

Source: Global Findex database.

Businesses generally lag behind governments when it comes to using digital payrolls. About 300 million account owners worldwide work in the private sector and get paid in cash, including 90 million in India. Indeed, India is one of several major developing economies where 10 percent or more of account owners receive private sector wage payments in cash; the share is almost twice as large in Indonesia, Myanmar, and Nepal (figure 6.10).

Large numbers of account owners receive cash payments for the sale of agricultural products —roughly 275 million in developing economies, including 15 million in Bangladesh and 80 million in China. The share of account owners receiving agricultural payments in cash is about 25 percent in Bangladesh, Uganda, and Uzbekistan—and 54 percent in Ethiopia (figure 6.11). Digitizing agricultural value chains offers multiple opportunities for increasing the use of accounts, not just through payments for the sale of agricultural products but also through important related payments, such as for purchases of crop insurance and agricultural inputs.

Globally, at least 145 million adults with an account receive payments from self-employment exclusively in cash. These include nearly 12 million account owners in Brazil and about 15 million in Indonesia. Digitizing these payments, and thus increasing their transparency, could provide financial service providers with information needed to extend and deepen access to financial services for both retailers and customers. Extending digital payments throughout the value chain of the consumer goods businesses that supply many small, self-employed merchants would also benefit distributors by improving the efficiency of payment collection and help to reinforce the use of digital payments throughout supply chains. Yet increasing the digitization of retail payments involves challenges, including the need to ensure that using digital payments for retail transactions is an attractive option for both merchants and customers.[16]

Arguably the single best way to increase account use would be to more fully digitize payments for water, electricity, and other utility bills. Globally, 1 billion adults with an account still pay utility bills in cash (map 6.7). In some economies people have the option of paying utility bills digitally but choose not to because of high fees, lack of proof of payment, or other concerns. If more utilities offered an attractive option for digital payments, efficiency could be improved on both sides. While about a quarter of account owners worldwide pay utility bills in cash, the share is higher in many major developing economies. About a third of account owners pay utility bills this way in China, Ethiopia, South Africa, and Turkey, and more than twice that share do so in Thailand and Vietnam. In Egypt 81 percent of account owners pay utility bills in cash (figure 6.12). And in both Brazil and Indonesia about 25 million women with an account still use cash to pay utility bills.

Digital technology could offer an alternative to cash for utility payments. Globally, about 910 million adults pay utility bills in cash despite having an account as well as a mobile phone. And roughly half a billion adults pay utility bills in cash even though they have an account, a mobile phone, and access to the internet. In Brazil, China, Peru, and Turkey about 60 percent of account owners who pay utility bills in cash have access to both a mobile phone and the internet. The shares are larger in Colombia and Vietnam, smaller in Egypt and South Africa.

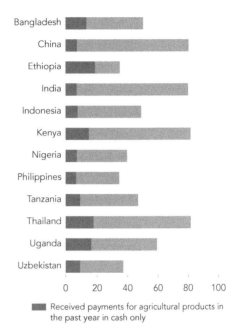

FIGURE 6.11

Millions of account owners receive payments for the sale of agricultural products in cash
Adults with an account (%), 2017

■ Received payments for agricultural products in the past year in cash only

Source: Global Findex database.

MAP 6.7
A billion adults who have an account still pay utility bills in cash
Adults with an account paying utility bills in the past year in cash only, 2017

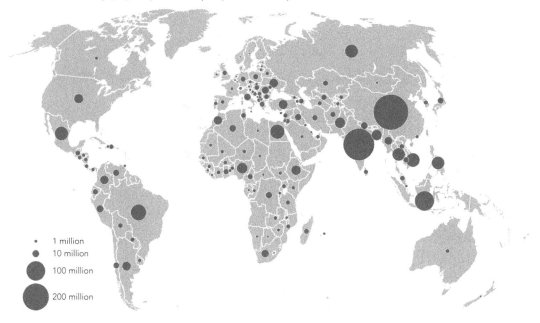

- 1 million
- 10 million
- 100 million
- 200 million

Source: Global Findex database.

Domestic remittances also offer potential for increasing the use of accounts. About 280 million account owners in developing economies use cash or an OTC service to send or receive domestic remittances. In Algeria and the Philippines roughly a quarter of account owners use one of these methods to do so (figure 6.13).

Formalizing saving is yet another way to increase account use. In developing economies 160 million account owners save semiformally, such as by using a savings club or savings collector to make regular savings payments, but not formally (by using an account at a financial institution). Semiformal saving is particularly widespread in Sub-Saharan Africa. About 25 percent of account owners save semiformally (but not formally) in Burkina Faso and Côte d'Ivoire, while about 33 percent do so in Cameroon and Uganda (figure 6.14). Elsewhere, in Indonesia and Pakistan about a fifth of account owners use semiformal (but not formal) savings methods.

Finally, wider acceptance of mobile payments could encourage greater use of accounts for retail transactions. This is especially true in economies where account owners are much more likely to have a mobile phone than a debit card, putting them in a position to leapfrog to mobile payments.[17] In India about

FIGURE 6.12
In many developing economies a third or more of account owners pay utility bills in cash
Adults with an account (%), 2017

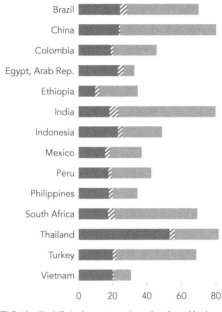

Paid utility bills in the past year in cash only and had a mobile phone

Paid utility bills in the past year in cash only and did not have a mobile phone

Sources: Global Findex database; Gallup World Poll 2017.

100 million adults with an inactive account have a debit card, while nearly 2.5 times as many— 240 million—have an inactive account plus a mobile phone. In both Russia and Thailand about 4 million adults have an inactive account and a debit card, while roughly twice as many have an inactive account as well as a mobile phone. Already equipped with an account and a mobile phone, these people might be inclined to use mobile payments if given attractive opportunities to do so.

FIGURE 6.13
Millions who have an account use other means to send or receive domestic remittances
Adults with an account (%), 2017

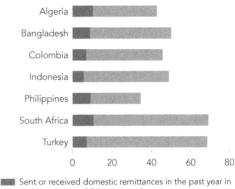

Sent or received domestic remittances in the past year in cash or using an OTC service only

Source: Global Findex database.

FIGURE 6.14
Millions of account owners save semiformally rather than by using their account
Adults with an account (%), 2017

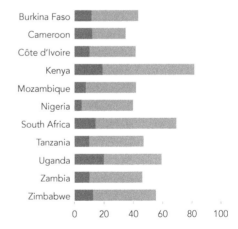

Saved semiformally but not formally in the past year

Source: Global Findex database.

Notes

1. For an overview, see Better Than Cash Alliance (2016); Demirgüç-Kunt, Klapper, and Singer (2017); and Klapper and Singer (2017).
2. Wright and others (2017).
3. Muralidharan, Niehaus, and Sukhtankar (2016).
4. See Karlan and others (2016).
5. See Klapper and Singer (2017).
6. Kendall and Voorhies (2014).
7. See Zimmerman and Baur (2016); and Stuart (2016).
8. See World Bank Group (2017).
9. See Miller and others (2014).
10. For a discussion of regulations to facilitate financial inclusion, see Claessens and Rojas-Suarez (2016).
11. See Demirgüç-Kunt and others (2017).
12. See Giné (2010).
13. Data on indicators that are part of the World Bank ID4D project were collected in collaboration with Gallup, Inc., and, like the Global Findex data, were collected only in economies where Gallup, Inc., conducts face-to-face interviews. This means that the data are available primarily for developing economies. In 13 high-income economies included in the 2017 Global Findex database, however, Gallup, Inc., conducts face-to-face rather than phone interviews, and in these economies data were collected for the ID4D indicators. Conversely, no data are available for the 4 developing economies included in the database where Gallup, Inc., conducts interviews by phone.
14. People may receive more than one type of government payment.
15. See World Bank Remittance Prices Worldwide Database (2017).
16. For additional discussion, see "Merchant Payments," Consultative Group to Assist the Poor, accessed March 27, 2018, http://www.cgap.org/about/people/merchant-payments.
17. See Zetterli and Pillai (2016).

REFERENCES

Aker, Jenny C., Rachid Boumnijel, Amanda McClelland, and Niall Tierney. 2016. "Payment Mechanisms and Anti-Poverty Programs: Evidence from a Mobile Money Cash Transfer Experiment in Niger." Tufts University Working Paper, Fletcher School and Department of Economics, Tufts University, Medford, MA.

Better Than Cash Alliance. 2016. "Accelerators to an Inclusive Digital Payments Ecosystem: Prioritization Framework and Guide." Better Than Cash Alliance, New York. https://www.betterthancash.org.

Brune, Lasse, Xavier Giné, Jessica Goldberg, and Dean Yang. 2016. "Facilitating Savings for Agriculture: Field Experimental Evidence from Malawi." *Economic Development and Cultural Change* 64 (2): 187–220.

Claessens, Stijn, and Liliana Rojas-Suarez. 2016. "Financial Regulations for Improving Financial Inclusion." CGD Task Force Report, Center for Global Development, Washington, DC.

Demirgüç-Kunt, Asli, Leora Klapper, Saniya Ansar, and Aditya Jagati. 2017. "Making It Easier to Apply for a Bank Account: A Study of the Indian Market." Policy Research Working Paper 8205, World Bank, Washington, DC.

Demirgüç-Kunt, Asli, Leora Klapper, and Dorothe Singer. 2017. "Financial Inclusion and Inclusive Growth: A Review of Recent Empirical Evidence." Policy Research Working Paper 8040, World Bank, Washington, DC.

Dupas, Pascaline, Dean Karlan, Jonathan Robinson, and Diego Ubfal. Forthcoming. "Banking the Unbanked? Evidence from Three Countries." *American Economic Journal: Applied Economics.*

Dupas, Pascaline, and Jonathan Robinson. 2013. "Savings Constraints and Microenterprise Development: Evidence from a Field Experiment in Kenya." *American Economic Journal: Applied Economics* 5 (1): 163–92.

Giné, Xavier. 2010. "Using Biometric Technology in Rural Credit Markets: The Case of Malawi." Finance & PSD Impact Evaluation Note, no. 11, World Bank, Washington, DC.

Jack, William, and Tavneet Suri. 2014. "Risk Sharing and Transactions Costs: Evidence from Kenya's Mobile Money Revolution." *American Economic Review* 104 (1): 183–223.

Karlan, Dean, Jake Kendall, Rebecca Mann, Rohini Pande, Tavneet Suri, and Jonathan Zinman. 2016. "Research and Impacts of Digital Financial Services." NBER Working Paper 22633, National Bureau of Economic Research, Cambridge, MA.

Kendall, Jake, and Rodger Voorhies. 2014. "The Mobile-Finance Revolution: How Cell Phones Can Spur Development." *Foreign Affairs* 93 (2): 9–13.

Klapper, Leora, and Dorothe Singer. 2017. "The Opportunities and Challenges of Digitizing Government-to-Person Payments." *World Bank Research Observer* 32 (2): 211–26.

Miller, Margaret, Julia Reichelstein, Christian Salas, and Bilal Zia. 2014. "Can You Help Someone Become Financially Capable? A Meta-Analysis of the Literature." Policy Research Working Paper 6745, World Bank, Washington, DC.

Muralidharan, Karthik, Paul Niehaus, and Sandip Sukhtankar. 2016. "Building State Capacity: Evidence from Biometric Smartcards in India." *American Economic Review* 106 (10): 2895–929.

Prina, Silvia. 2015. "Banking the Poor via Savings Accounts: Evidence from a Field Experiment." *Journal of Development Economics* 115 (July): 16–31.

Schaner, Simone. 2017. "The Cost of Convenience? Transaction Costs, Bargaining Power, and Savings Account Use in Kenya." *Journal of Human Resources* 52 (4): 919–45.

Stuart, Guy. 2016. "Government-to-Person Transfers: On-Ramp to Financial Inclusion?" Center for Financial Inclusion, Washington, DC.

Suri, Tavneet, and William Jack. 2016. "The Long-Run Poverty and Gender Impacts of Mobile Money." *Science* 354 (6317): 1288–92.

World Bank Group. 2017. *Good Practices for Financial Consumer Protection, 2017 Edition.* Washington, DC: World Bank.

World Bank Remittance Prices Worldwide Database. 2017. "Remittance Prices Worldwide: An Analysis of Trends in Cost of Remittance Services." Issue 24. World Bank, Washington, DC.

Wright, Richard, Erdal Tekin, Volkan Topalli, Chandler McClellan, Timothy Dickinson, and Richard Rosenfeld. 2017. "Less Cash, Less Crime: Evidence from the Electronic Benefit Transfer Program." *Journal of Law and Economics* 60 (2): 361–83.

Zetterli, Peter, and Rashmi Pillai. 2016. "Digitizing Merchant Payments: What Will It Take?" CGAP Note, Consultative Group to Assist the Poor, Washington, DC.

Zimmerman, Jamie M., and Silvia Baur. 2016. "Understanding How Consumer Risks in Digital Social Payments Can Erode Their Financial Inclusion Potential." CGAP Brief, Consultative Group to Assist the Poor, Washington, DC.

SURVEY METHODOLOGY

The indicators in the 2017 Global Findex database are drawn from survey data covering almost 150,000 people in 144 economies—representing more than 97 percent of the world's population (see table A.1 for a list of the economies included). The survey was carried out over the 2017 calendar year by Gallup, Inc., as part of its Gallup World Poll, which since 2005 has annually conducted surveys of approximately 1,000 people in each of more than 160 economies and in over 150 languages, using randomly selected, nationally representative samples. The target population is the entire civilian, noninstitutionalized population age 15 and above.

Interview procedure

Surveys are conducted face to face in economies where telephone coverage represents less than 80 percent of the population or where this is the customary methodology. In most economies the fieldwork is completed in two to four weeks.

In economies where face-to-face surveys are conducted, the first stage of sampling is the identification of primary sampling units. These units are stratified by population size, geography, or both, and clustering is achieved through one or more stages of sampling. Where population information is available, sample selection is based on probabilities proportional to population size; otherwise, simple random sampling is used.

Random route procedures are used to select sampled households. Unless an outright refusal occurs, interviewers make up to three attempts to survey the sampled household. To increase the probability of contact and completion, attempts are made at different times of the day and, where possible, on different days. If an interview cannot be obtained at the initial sampled household, a simple substitution method is used.

Respondents are randomly selected within the selected households. Each eligible household member is listed and the handheld survey device randomly selects the household member to be interviewed. For paper surveys, the Kish grid method is used to select the respondent.[1] In economies where cultural restrictions dictate gender matching, respondents are randomly selected from among all eligible adults of the interviewer's gender.

In economies where telephone interviewing is employed, random digit dialing or a nationally representative list of phone numbers is used. In most economies where cell phone penetration is high, a dual sampling frame is used. Random selection of respondents is achieved by using either the latest birthday or household enumeration method. At least three attempts are made to reach a person in each household, spread over different days and times of day.

Data preparation

Data weighting is used to ensure a nationally representative sample for each economy. Final weights consist of the base sampling weight, which corrects for unequal probability of selection based on household size, and the poststratification weight, which corrects for sampling and nonresponse error. Poststratification weights use economy-level population statistics on gender and age and, where reliable data are available, education or socioeconomic status.

Table A.1 shows the data collection period, number of interviews, approximate design effect, and margin of error for each economy as well as sampling details where relevant.

Additional information about the Global Findex data, including the complete database, can be found at http://www.worldbank.org/globalfindex.

Additional information about the methodology used in the Gallup World Poll can be found at http://www.gallup.com/178667/gallup-world-poll-work.aspx.

Note

1. The Kish grid is a table of numbers used to select the interviewee. First, the interviewer lists the name, gender, and age of all permanent household members age 15 and above, whether or not they are present, in order by age. Second, the interviewer finds the column number of the Kish grid that corresponds to the last digit of the questionnaire and the row number for the number of eligible household members. The number in the cell where the column and row intersect is the person selected for the interview.

Details of survey methodology for economies included in the 2017 Global Findex survey and database

Economy	Region[a]	Income group	Data collection period	Interviews	Design effect[b]	Margin of error[c]	Mode of interviewing	Languages	Exclusions and other sampling details
Afghanistan	SAS	Low	May 22–Jun 20, 2017	1,000	1.47	3.8	Face to face	Dari, Pashto	Gender-matched sampling was used during the final stage of selection.
Albania	ECA	Upper middle	May 18–Jun 12, 2017	1,000	1.30	3.5	Face to face[d]	Albanian	
Algeria	MNA	Upper middle	Sep 11–Sep 26, 2017	1,016	1.44	3.7	Face to face[d]	Arabic	Sample excludes sparsely populated areas in the far South, representing about 10% of the population.
Argentina	LAC	Upper middle	Jun 22–Aug 14, 2017	1,000	1.37	3.6	Face to face[d]	Spanish	Sample excludes dispersed rural population areas, representing about 5.7% of the population.
Armenia	ECA	Lower middle	Jun 6–Jun 29, 2017	1,000	1.28	3.5	Face to face[d]	Armenian	
Australia	HI	High	Apr 28–Jul 17, 2017	1,008	2.19	4.6	Landline and cellular telephone	English	
Austria	HI	High	May 30–Jun 28, 2017	1,000	1.29	3.5	Landline and cellular telephone	German	
Azerbaijan	ECA	Upper middle	Jul 25–Aug 15, 2017	1,000	1.41	3.7	Face to face[d]	Azeri, Russian	Sample excludes Kelbadjaro-Lacha, Nagorno-Karabakh, and Nakhichevan territories, representing about 14% of the population.
Bahrain	HI	High	May 2–May 20, 2017	1,060	1.44	3.6	Landline and cellular telephone	Arabic, English	Sample includes only Bahraini nationals, Arab expatriates, and non-Arabs who were able to participate in the survey in Arabic or English.
Bangladesh	SAS	Lower middle	Apr 18–May 4, 2017	1,000	1.34	3.6	Face to face[d]	Bengali	Sample excludes three hill districts in Chittagong (Bandarban, Khagrachori, and Rangamati) for security reasons. The excluded areas represent about 1% of the population.
Belarus	ECA	Upper middle	Jun 24–Jul 18, 2017	1,053	1.39	3.6	Face to face[d]	Russian	
Belgium	HI	High	Jul 11–Sep 18, 2017	1,001	1.42	3.7	Landline and cellular telephone	French, Dutch	
Benin	SSA	Low	May 1–May 14, 2017	1,000	1.53	3.8	Face to face[d]	Bariba, Fon, French, Anago	
Bolivia	LAC	Lower middle	Jul 2–Sep 20, 2017	1,000	1.44	3.7	Face to face[d]	Spanish	
Bosnia and Herzegovina	ECA	Upper middle	May 19–Jun 14, 2017	1,000	1.28	3.5	Face to face[d]	Bosnian, Croatian, Serbian	
Botswana	SSA	Upper middle	May 21–Jun 7, 2017	1,000	1.54	3.8	Face to face[d]	English, Setswana	

Economy	Region[a]	Income group	Data collection period	Interviews	Design effect[b]	Margin of error[c]	Mode of interviewing	Languages	Exclusions and other sampling details
Brazil	LAC	Upper middle	May 11–Jun 15, 2017	1,000	1.39	3.7	Face to face[d]	Portuguese	
Bulgaria	ECA	Upper middle	May 11–Jun 26, 2017	1,000	1.49	3.8	Face to face[d]	Bulgarian	
Burkina Faso	SSA	Low	May 16–May 29, 2017	1,000	1.63	4.0	Face to face[d]	Dioula, French, Fulfulde, Moore	
Cambodia	EAP	Lower middle	Mar 18–Apr 8, 2017	1,600	1.42	2.9	Face to face[d]	Khmer	
Cameroon	SSA	Lower middle	Feb 21–Mar 7, 2017	1,000	1.45	3.7	Face to face[d]	French, English, Fulfulde	Sample excludes some localities because of security concerns: Blangoua, Bourrha, Darak, Fotokol, Goulfey, Hile-Alifa, Kolofata, Koza, Mayo Moskota, Mogode, Mora, Tokombere, Waza, and Zina. The excluded areas represent about 10% of the population.
Canada	HI	High	Aug 10–Nov 29, 2017	1,003	1.58	3.9	Landline and cellular telephone	English, French	
Central African Republic	SSA	Low	May 21–Jun 5, 2017	1,000	1.56	3.9	Face to face[d]	French, Sangho	Sample excludes some prefectures because of security concerns: Bamingui-Bangoran, Basse-Kotto, Haute-Kotto, Haut-Mbomou, Mbomou, Nana-Grébizi, Ouham, Ouham-Pende, and Vakaga. The excluded areas represent about 40% of the estimated population.
Chad	SSA	Low	Apr 17–May 4, 2017	1,000	1.65	4.0	Face to face[d]	French, Chadian Arabic, Ngambaye	Sample excludes seven regions because of security concerns and wilderness (Bourkou, Ennedi, Ouaddai, Salamat, Sila, Tibesti, and Wadi Fira) as well as quartiers or villages with less than 50 inhabitants. The excluded areas represent about 20% of the population.
Chile	HI	High	Jul 8–Aug 10, 2017	1,040	1.59	3.8	Face to face[d]	Spanish	Sample excludes the remote areas Antarctica, Easter Island, and Juan Fernández Island, representing about 0.04% of the population.
China	EAP	Upper middle	May 14–Jul 7, 2017	3,627	1.53	2.0	Face to face	Chinese	Sample excludes Tibet and Xinjiang, representing less than 5% of the population. Unless otherwise noted, data for China do not include data for Hong Kong SAR, China; Macao SAR, China; or Taiwan, China.
Colombia	LAC	Upper middle	Jun 16–Jul 5, 2017	1,000	1.32	3.6	Face to face[d]	Spanish	

Economy	Region[a]	Income group	Data collection period	Interviews	Design effect[b]	Margin of error[c]	Mode of interviewing	Languages	Exclusions and other sampling details
Congo, Dem. Rep.	SSA	Low	Mar 25–Apr 15, 2017	1,000	1.51	3.8	Face to face[d]	French, Kituba, Lingala	Sample excludes parts of several provinces (Eastern Kasai, Equateur, Katanga, North Kivu, Orientale, and South Kivu) and all of Western Kasai province for security reasons. The excluded areas represent about 34% of the estimated population.
Congo, Rep.	SSA	Lower middle	May 6–May 31, 2017	1,000	1.65	4.0	Face to face[d]	French, Lingala, Kikongo, Swahili, Tshiluba	
Costa Rica	LAC	Upper middle	Apr 19–Jul 1, 2017	1,000	1.48	3.8	Face to face[d]	Spanish	
Côte d'Ivoire	SSA	Lower middle	May 14–May 30, 2017	1,000	1.56	3.9	Face to face[d]	French, Dioula	
Croatia	ECA	Upper middle	May 23–Jul 9, 2017	1,000	1.38	3.6	Face to face[d]	Croatian	
Cyprus	HI	High	Apr 27–Jun 20, 2017	1,023	1.39	3.6	Landline and cellular telephone	Greek, English	
Czech Republic	HI	High	Apr 4–Jul 11, 2017	1,000	1.28	3.5	Face to face[d]	Czech	
Denmark	HI	High	May 5–May 30, 2017	1,000	1.30	3.5	Landline and cellular telephone	Danish	
Dominican Republic	LAC	Upper middle	Jul 11–Jul 28, 2017	1,000	1.43	3.7	Face to face[d]	Spanish	
Ecuador	LAC	Upper middle	Jun 10–Jul 6, 2017	1,000	1.32	3.6	Face to face[d]	Spanish	
Egypt, Arab Rep.	MNA	Lower middle	May 16–May 26, 2017	1,000	1.24	3.4	Face to face[d]	Arabic	Sample excludes frontier governorates (Matruh, New Valley, North Sinai, Red Sea, and South Sinai) because of their remoteness and small population share. The excluded areas represent less than 2% of the population.
El Salvador	LAC	Lower middle	May 20–Jun 13, 2017	1,000	1.59	3.9	Face to face[d]	Spanish	
Estonia	HI	High	Jun 15–Jul 15, 2017	1,000	1.21	3.4	Face to face[d]	Estonian, Russian	
Ethiopia	SSA	Low	May 2–Jun 26, 2017	1,000	1.40	3.7	Face to face[d]	Amharic, Oromo, Tigrinya	
Finland	HI	High	Apr 26–May 30, 2017	1,000	1.35	3.6	Cellular telephone	Finnish, Swedish	
France	HI	High	Apr 19–May 18, 2017	1,000	1.41	3.7	Landline and cellular telephone	French	
Gabon	SSA	Upper middle	Jun 14–Jul 5, 2017	1,000	1.55	3.9	Face to face[d]	French, Fang, Punu	
Georgia	ECA	Lower middle	Jun 9–Jun 29, 2017	1,000	1.32	3.6	Face to face[d]	Georgian, Russian	

Economy	Regiona	Income group	Data collection period	Interviews	Design effectb	Margin of errorc	Mode of interviewing	Languages	Exclusions and other sampling details
Germany	HI	High	Apr 19–May 18, 2017	1,000	1.40	3.7	Landline and cellular telephone	German	
Ghana	SSA	Lower middle	May 20–Jun 10, 2017	1,000	1.36	3.6	Face to faced	English, Ewe, Hausa, Twi, Dagbani	
Greece	HI	High	May 20–Jun 16, 2017	1,000	1.30	3.5	Face to faced	Greek	
Guatemala	LAC	Lower middle	May 17–Jun 12, 2017	1,000	1.26	3.5	Face to faced	Spanish	
Guinea	SSA	Low	Jul 10–Jul 27, 2017	1,000	1.43	3.7	Face to faced	French, Malinke, Pular, Soussou	
Haiti	LAC	Low	Jul 13–Jul 22, 2017	504	1.27	4.9	Face to faced	Creole	
Honduras	LAC	Lower middle	May 24–Jun 18, 2017	1,000	1.45	3.7	Face to faced	Spanish	
Hong Kong SAR, China	HI	High	Apr 27–Jul 8, 2017	1,007	1.37	3.6	Landline and cellular telephone	Chinese	
Hungary	HI	High	May 14–Jun 21, 2017	1,000	1.36	3.6	Face to faced	Hungarian	
India	SAS	Lower middle	Apr 21–Jun 2, 2017	3,000	1.48	2.2	Face to faced	Assamese, Bengali, Gujarati, Hindi, Kannada, Malayalam, Marathi, Odia, Punjabi, Tamil, Telugu	Sample excludes Northeast states and remote islands, representing less than 10% of the population.
Indonesia	EAP	Lower middle	Apr 10–May 20, 2017	1,000	1.38	3.6	Face to faced	Bahasa Indonesia	
Iran, Islamic Rep.	MNA	Upper middle	May 23–Jun 15, 2017	1,004	1.65	4.0	Landline and cellular telephone	Farsi	
Iraq	MNA	Upper middle	May 15–Jun 9, 2017	1,000	1.51	3.8	Landline and cellular telephone	Arabic, Kurdish	
Ireland	HI	High	Mar 14–Apr 10, 2017	1,000	1.22	3.4	Landline and cellular telephone	English	
Israel	HI	High	May 24–Jun 22, 2017	1,000	1.12	3.3	Face to face	Hebrew, Russian, Arabic	Sample excludes East Jerusalem. This area is included in the sample for West Bank and Gaza.
Italy	HI	High	Jan 30–Feb 23, 2017	1,000	1.49	3.8	Landline and cellular telephone	Italian	
Japan	HI	High	Apr 5–Jul 9, 2017	1,005	1.46	3.7	Landline and cellular telephone	Japanese	Landline random-digit-dial sample excludes 12 municipalities near the nuclear power plant in Fukushima, representing less than 1% of the population.
Jordan	MNA	Lower middle	Apr 25–Jul 10, 2017	1,012	1.30	3.5	Face to faced	Arabic	Sample includes any respondent in a fixed household able to participate in the survey in Arabic. This resulted in a higher percentage of self-reported non-Jordanians in the 2017 sample (12%, compared with less than 5% in previous waves).

Economy	Region[a]	Income group	Data collection period	Interviews	Design effect[b]	Margin of error[c]	Mode of interviewing	Languages	Exclusions and other sampling details
Kazakhstan	ECA	Upper middle	Jun 5–Jul 2, 2017	1,000	1.42	3.7	Face to face[d]	Russian, Kazakh	
Kenya	SSA	Lower middle	Mar 11–Mar 24, 2017	1,000	1.53	3.8	Face to face[d]	English, Swahili	
Korea, Rep.	HI	High	Mar 29–Jul 5, 2017	1,000	1.47	3.8	Landline and cellular telephone	Korean	
Kosovo	ECA	Lower middle	May 15–Jun 16, 2017	1,000	1.30	3.5	Face to face[d]	Albanian, Serbian	
Kuwait	HI	High	May 18–Jun 5, 2017	1,000	1.34	3.6	Landline and cellular telephone	Arabic, English	Sample includes only Kuwaitis, Arab expatriates, and non-Arabs who were able to complete the interview in Arabic or English.
Kyrgyz Republic	ECA	Lower middle	Jul 10–Jul 25, 2017	1,000	1.04	3.2	Face to face[d]	Kyrgyz, Russian, Uzbek	
Lao PDR	EAP	Lower middle	Sep 1–Sep 27, 2017	1,000	1.33	3.6	Face to face[d]	Lao	Sample excludes Xaisomboun Province and some communes in Bokeo, Huaphanh, Luangnamtha, Luangprabang, Oudomxay, Phongsaly, Saravane, Sekong, Xayaboury, and Xienkhuang because of remoteness or security issues. The excluded areas represent about 10% of the population.
Latvia	HI	High	Jun 5–Jul 27, 2017	1,002	1.30	3.5	Face to face[d]	Latvian, Russian	
Lebanon	MNA	Upper middle	Apr 20–May 29, 2017	1,000	1.37	3.6	Face to face[d]	Arabic	Sample excludes towns of Baalbek, Bint Jbeil, and Hermel under the control of Hezbollah as well as the Beirut suburb of Dahiyeh. The excluded areas represent about 13% of the population. Excluded zones were replaced by areas within the same governorate.
Lesotho	SSA	Lower middle	Oct 26–Nov 10, 2017	1,000	1.45	3.7	Face to face[d]	English, Sotho	
Liberia	SSA	Low	May 31–Jul 4, 2017	1,000	1.32	3.6	Face to face[d]	English, Pidgin English	
Libya	MNA	Upper middle	May 17–May 27, 2017	1,002	1.80	4.2	Cellular telephone	Arabic	
Lithuania	HI	High	Jul 17–Aug 6, 2017	1,000	1.36	3.6	Face to face[d]	Lithuanian	
Luxembourg	HI	High	Apr 19–May 18, 2017	1,000	1.45	3.7	Landline and cellular telephone	French, German	
Macedonia, FYR	ECA	Upper middle	Jun 4–Jul 26, 2017	1,008	1.43	3.7	Face to face[d]	Macedonian, Albanian	
Madagascar	SSA	Low	Mar 28–May 2, 2017	1,000	1.55	3.9	Face to face[d]	French, Malagasy	Sample excludes unsafe or inaccessible regions, representing about 25% of the population.

Economy	Region[a]	Income group	Data collection period	Interviews	Design effect[b]	Margin of error[c]	Mode of interviewing	Languages	Exclusions and other sampling details
Malawi	SSA	Low	May 22–Jun 1, 2017	1,000	1.37	3.6	Face to face[d]	Chichewa, English, Tumbuka	
Malaysia	EAP	Upper middle	May 9, 2017–Jan 2, 2018	1,004	1.63	3.9	Landline and cellular telephone	Bahasa Malay, Chinese, English	
Mali	SSA	Low	Jul 23–Aug 6, 2017	1,000	1.52	3.8	Face to face[d]	French, Bambara	Sample excludes the regions of Gao, Kidal, Mopti, and Tombouctou because of security concerns. These regions represent 23% of the population.
Malta	HI	High	Mar 17–Apr 15, 2017	1,003	1.57	3.9	Landline and cellular telephone	Maltese, English	
Mauritania	SSA	Lower middle	Mar 27–Apr 7, 2017	1,000	1.64	4.0	Face to face[d]	French, Poulaar, Wolof, Hassanya	
Mauritius	SSA	Upper middle	Apr 19–May 31, 2017	1,000	1.43	3.7	Landline and cellular telephone	Creole, English, French	
Mexico	LAC	Upper middle	Jun 8–Jul 8, 2017	1,000	1.46	3.7	Face to face	Spanish	
Moldova	ECA	Lower middle	Jul 21–Aug 8, 2017	1,000	1.18	3.4	Face to face[d]	Romanian, Russian	Sample excludes Transnistria (Prednestrovie) because of security concerns. The excluded area represents about 13% of the population.
Mongolia	EAP	Lower middle	May 25–Jun 30, 2017	1,000	1.24	3.5	Face to face[d]	Mongolian	
Montenegro	ECA	Upper middle	May 12–Jun 15, 2017	1,000	1.41	3.7	Face to face[d]	Montenegrin, Serbian	Sampling frame excluded some very small and remote villages (with less than 150 people), representing about 0.5–1.5% of the population.
Morocco	MNA	Lower middle	Oct 20–Dec 15, 2017	5,110	1.54	1.7	Face to face[d]	Moroccan Arabic	An equal sample size was used for each region (disproportionate sampling). Data were weighted to population distribution.
Mozambique	SSA	Low	Jun 2–Aug 22, 2017	1,000	1.48	3.8	Face to face[d]	Portuguese, Xichangana, Cisena, Emakhuwa	
Myanmar	EAP	Lower middle	Mar 18–Apr 3, 2017	1,600	1.30	2.8	Face to face[d]	Burmese	Sample excludes Chin, Kachin, and Kayah states, representing less than 5% of the population.
Namibia	SSA	Upper middle	May 23–Jul 26, 2017	1,000	1.49	3.8	Face to face[d]	English, Oshivambo	
Nepal	SAS	Low	Aug 10–Sep 12, 2017	1,000	1.45	3.7	Face to face[d]	Nepali	
Netherlands	HI	High	Jul 11–Sep 1, 2017	1,000	1.40	3.7	Landline and cellular telephone	Dutch	
New Zealand	HI	High	Feb 18–Apr 28, 2017	1,000	1.50	3.8	Landline and cellular telephone	English	

Economy	Region[a]	Income group	Data collection period	Interviews	Design effect[b]	Margin of error[c]	Mode of interviewing	Languages	Exclusions and other sampling details
Nicaragua	LAC	Lower middle	May 10–Jun 15, 2017	1,000	1.55	3.9	Face to face[d]	Spanish	
Niger	SSA	Low	Apr 28–May 11, 2017	1,000	1.50	3.8	Face to face[d]	French, Hausa, Zarma	
Nigeria	SSA	Lower middle	Apr 4–Apr 28, 2017	1,000	1.55	3.9	Face to face[d]	English, Hausa, Igbo, Pidgin English, Yoruba	Sample excludes the states of Adamawa, Borno, and Yobe because of security concerns. These states represent 7% of the population.
Norway	HI	High	Apr 28–May 30, 2017	1,000	1.43	3.7	Landline and cellular telephone	Norwegian	
Pakistan	SAS	Lower middle	Mar 20–May 3, 2017	1,600	1.43	2.9	Face to face[d]	Urdu	
Panama	LAC	Upper middle	May 9–Jun 5, 2017	1,000	1.47	3.8	Face to face[d]	Spanish	
Paraguay	LAC	Upper middle	Dec 15, 2017–Jan 18, 2018	1,000	1.30	3.5	Face to face[d]	Spanish, Jeporá	
Peru	LAC	Upper middle	Jul 1–Jul 25, 2017	1,000	1.48	3.8	Face to face[d]	Spanish	
Philippines	EAP	Lower middle	Jul 16–Aug 7, 2017	1,000	1.41	3.7	Face to face[d]	Filipino, Iluko, Hiligaynon, Cebuano, Masbatenyo, Waray, Tausug	
Poland	HI	High	Aug 12–Sep 25, 2017	1,000	1.32	3.6	Face to face[d]	Polish	
Portugal	HI	High	Mar 27–May 3, 2017	1,002	1.43	3.7	Landline and cellular telephone	Portuguese	
Romania	ECA	Upper middle	Apr 12–Jun 15, 2017	1,001	1.46	3.7	Face to face[d]	Romanian, Hungarian	
Russian Federation	ECA	Upper middle	Jun 9–Aug 20, 2017	2,000	1.35	2.5	Face to face[d]	Russian	Sample excludes remote or difficult-to-access areas in the Far North, North Caucasus, and Far East (Nenets autonomous region, Yamalo-Nenets autonomous region, Chukotsk region) as well as other remote or difficult-to-access districts. The excluded areas represent about 20% of the population.
Rwanda	SSA	Low	Dec 7–Dec 20, 2017	1,000	1.32	3.6	Face to face[d]	Kinyarwanda, English	
Saudi Arabia	HI	High	Apr 30–May 20, 2017	1,009	1.43	3.7	Landline and cellular telephone	Arabic, English	Sample includes only Saudi nationals, Arab expatriates, and non-Arabs who were able to participate in the survey in Arabic or English.
Senegal	SSA	Low	Mar 27–Apr 9, 2017	1,000	1.36	3.6	Face to face[d]	French, Wolof	
Serbia	ECA	Upper middle	May 15–Jun 27, 2017	1,000	1.38	3.6	Face to face[d]	Serbian	

Economy	Regionª	Income group	Data collection period	Interviews	Design effectᵇ	Margin of errorᶜ	Mode of interviewing	Languages	Exclusions and other sampling details
Sierra Leone	SSA	Low	Mar 25–Apr 11, 2017	1,000	1.36	3.6	Face to faceᵈ	English, Krio, Mende	
Singapore	HI	High	May 17–Aug 9, 2017	1,000	1.39	3.7	Face to face	English, Chinese, Bahasa Malay	Condominiums were covered on a best-effort basis; 7% of condo dwellers were excluded from the survey. About 14% of the population were living in condominiums as of 2016.
Slovak Republic	HI	High	May 12–Jun 6, 2017	1,000	1.36	3.6	Face to faceᵈ	Hungarian, Slovak	
Slovenia	HI	High	Mar 3–Apr 5, 2017	1,000	1.50	3.8	Landline and cellular telephone	Slovene	
South Africa	SSA	Upper middle	Jun 20–Jul 5, 2017	1,000	1.41	3.7	Face to faceᵈ	Afrikaans, English, Sotho, Xhosa, Zulu	
South Sudan	SSA	Low	Jun 21–Jul 23, 2017	1,000	1.50	3.8	Face to faceᵈ	Arabic, Bari, Dinka, English, Juba Arabic, Nuer, Zande	Sample excludes parts of 9 of 10 states because of security concerns. It excludes the majority of Unity State and Upper Nile State as well as all of Jonglei State except Bor South County. The excluded areas represent 44% of the population.
Spain	HI	High	Jan 30–Feb 23, 2017	1,000	1.62	3.9	Landline and cellular telephone	Spanish	
Sri Lanka	SAS	Lower middle	Jun 28–Aug 10, 2017	1,104	1.55	3.7	Face to faceᵈ	Sinhala, Tamil	
Sweden	HI	High	May 3–May 30, 2017	1,000	1.50	3.8	Landline and cellular telephone	Swedish	
Switzerland	HI	High	Apr 19–May 18, 2017	1,000	1.40	3.7	Landline and cellular telephone	German, French, Italian	
Taiwan, China	HI	High	Apr 10–Jun 11, 2017	1,000	1.47	3.8	Landline and cellular telephone	Chinese	
Tajikistan	ECA	Lower middle	Jun 15–Jul 11, 2017	1,000	1.36	3.6	Face to faceᵈ	Tajik	
Tanzania	SSA	Low	Jul 16–Jul 30, 2017	1,000	1.53	3.8	Face to faceᵈ	English, Swahili	
Thailand	EAP	Upper middle	Jun 6–Sep 26, 2017	1,000	1.53	3.8	Face to face	Thai	Sample excludes three provinces in the South region (Narathiwat, Pattani, and Yala) for security reasons as well as a few districts in other provinces. The excluded areas represent less than 4% of the population.
Togo	SSA	Low	Jun 20–Jul 1, 2017	1,000	1.69	4.0	Face to faceᵈ	French, Ewe, Kabiye	
Trinidad and Tobago	HI	High	Jul 17–Oct 10, 2017	504	1.52	5.4	Face to faceᵈ	English	
Tunisia	MNA	Lower middle	Apr 11–Apr 25, 2017	1,001	1.20	3.4	Face to faceᵈ	Arabic	

Economy	Region[a]	Income group	Data collection period	Interviews	Design effect[b]	Margin of error[c]	Mode of interviewing	Languages	Exclusions and other sampling details
Turkey	ECA	Upper middle	May 15–Jun 16, 2017	1,000	1.46	3.7	Face to face[d]	Turkish	
Turkmenistan	ECA	Upper middle	Jun 2–Jun 15, 2017	1,000	1.24	3.5	Face to face[d]	Turkmen, Russian	
Uganda	SSA	Low	Jul 19–Jul 29, 2017	1,000	1.41	3.7	Face to face[d]	Ateso, English, Luganda, Runyankole	
Ukraine	ECA	Lower middle	May 30–Jul 20, 2017	1,000	1.46	3.7	Face to face[d]	Russian, Ukrainian	Sample excludes occupied and conflict areas in Donetsk and Lugansk oblasts. The excluded areas represent 10% of the population.
United Arab Emirates	HI	High	Jul 2–Jul 30, 2017	1,003	1.21	3.4	Landline and cellular telephone	Arabic, English	Sample includes only Emirati nationals, Arab expatriates, and non-Arabs who were able to participate in the survey in Arabic or English.
United Kingdom	HI	High	Mar 14–Apr 10, 2017	1,000	1.37	3.6	Landline and cellular telephone	English	
United States	HI	High	Aug 9–Sep 12, 2017	1,005	1.56	3.9	Landline and cellular telephone	English, Spanish	
Uruguay	HI	High	Jul 4–Aug 21, 2017	1,000	1.41	3.7	Face to face[d]	Spanish	
Uzbekistan	ECA	Lower middle	Jun 2–Jun 29, 2017	1,000	1.38	3.6	Face to face[d]	Uzbek, Russian	
Venezuela, RB	LAC	Upper middle	Aug 26–Nov 15, 2017	1,000	1.69	4.0	Face to face[d]	Spanish	Sample excludes the Federal Dependencies because of remoteness and difficulty of access, as well as some additional areas because of security concerns. The excluded areas represent about 5% of the population.
Vietnam	EAP	Lower middle	Sep 25–Oct 15, 2017	1,002	1.33	3.6	Face to face[d]	Vietnamese	Sample excludes 11 provinces: An Giang, Dac Lak, Dien Bien, Gia Lai, Ha Giang, Ha Tinh, Kien Giang, Kon Tum, Nghe An, Quang Binh, and Thanh Hoa. The excluded areas represent about 19% of the population.
West Bank and Gaza	MNA	Lower middle	May 10–May 29, 2017	1,000	1.48	3.8	Face to face[d]	Arabic	Sample excludes areas with security concerns close to the Israeli borders, areas accessible only to special Israeli permit holders, and areas with a population of less than 1,000. The excluded areas represent less than 2% of the population. The sample includes East Jerusalem.
Zambia	SSA	Lower middle	Jun 20–Jul 16, 2017	1,000	1.37	3.6	Face to face[d]	Bemba, English, Lozi, Nyanja, Tonga	
Zimbabwe	SSA	Low	Apr 8–May 8, 2017	1,000	1.42	3.7	Face to face[d]	English, Shona, Ndebele	

Source: Data on survey methodology provided by Gallup, Inc. For more details, see http://www.gallup.com/178667/gallup-world-poll-work.aspx.

a. Regions exclude high-income economies (HI) and may differ from common geographic usage. EAP = East Asia and the Pacific; ECA = Europe and Central Asia; LAC = Latin America and the Caribbean; MNA = Middle East and North Africa; SAS = South Asia; SSA = Sub-Saharan Africa.
b. The design effect calculation reflects the weights and does not incorporate the intraclass correlation coefficients because they vary by question. Design effect calculation: n*(sum of squared weights)/[(sum of weights)*(sum of weights)].
c. The margin of error is calculated around a proportion at the 95 percent confidence level. The maximum margin of error was calculated assuming a reported percentage of 50 percent and takes into account the design effect. Margin of error calculation: $\sqrt{(0.25/N)}*1.96*\sqrt{(DE)}$. Other errors that can affect survey validity include measurement error associated with the questionnaire, such as translation issues, and coverage error, where a part of the target population has a zero probability of being selected for the survey.
d. Interviewers used a handheld device (computer-assisted personal interviewing, or CAPI) during the interviews rather than pen and paper.

INDICATOR TABLE

Economy	Account ownership, 2017		
	Adults with an account (%)	Gap between men and women (percentage points)[a]	Gap between richer and poorer (percentage points)[b]
Afghanistan	15	15	—
Albania	40	4	29
Algeria	43	27	13
Argentina	49	−4	18
Armenia	48	15	22
Australia	100	—	—
Austria	98	—	—
Azerbaijan	29	—	17
Bahrain	83	11	11
Bangladesh	50	29	17
Belarus	81	—	11
Belgium	99	—	—
Benin	38	20	11
Bolivia	54	—	19
Bosnia and Herzegovina	59	8	19
Botswana	51	9	27
Brazil	70	5	22
Bulgaria	72	—	29
Burkina Faso	43	17	27
Cambodia	22	—	12
Cameroon	35	9	16
Canada	100	—	—
Central African Republic	14	8	8
Chad	22	14	13
Chile	74	6	12
China	80	8	20
Colombia	46	7	18
Congo, Dem. Rep.	26	—	14
Congo, Rep.	26	10	13
Costa Rica	68	15	16
Côte d'Ivoire	41	11	12
Croatia	86	7	9
Cyprus	89	—	8
Czech Republic	81	5	17

Economy	Account ownership, 2017		
	Adults with an account (%)	Gap between men and women (percentage points)[a]	Gap between richer and poorer (percentage points)[b]
Denmark	100	—	—
Dominican Republic	56	4	23
Ecuador	51	18	30
Egypt, Arab Rep.	33	12	21
El Salvador	30	13	18
Estonia	98	—	—
Ethiopia	35	12	21
Finland	100	—	—
France	94	6	—
Gabon	59	10	15
Georgia	61	−5	25
Germany	99	—	—
Ghana	58	8	16
Greece	85	—	7
Guatemala	44	4	23
Guinea	23	8	6
Haiti	33	5	25
Honduras	45	9	20
Hong Kong SAR, China	95	—	5
Hungary	75	6	12
India	80	6	5
Indonesia	49	−5	20
Iran, Islamic Rep.	94	5	—
Iraq	23	6	7
Ireland	95	—	4
Israel	93	—	12
Italy	94	5	5
Japan	98	—	—
Jordan	42	30	16
Kazakhstan	59	—	16
Kenya	82	8	18
Korea, Rep.	95	—	5
Kosovo	52	17	13
Kuwait	80	10	15
Kyrgyz Republic	40	—	7
Lao PDR	29	−6	19
Latvia	93	—	8
Lebanon	45	24	25
Lesotho	46	—	22
Liberia	36	15	15
Libya	66	11	12
Lithuania	83	4	8
Luxembourg	99	—	—
Macedonia, FYR	77	7	16
Madagascar	18	—	9

Economy	Account ownership, 2017		
	Adults with an account (%)	Gap between men and women (percentage points)[a]	Gap between richer and poorer (percentage points)[b]
Malawi	34	8	21
Malaysia	85	5	8
Mali	35	20	7
Malta	97	—	4
Mauritania	21	11	13
Mauritius	90	6	6
Mexico	37	8	18
Moldova	44	—	20
Mongolia	93	−4	4
Montenegro	68	—	13
Morocco	29	25	16
Mozambique	42	18	25
Myanmar	26	—	6
Namibia	81	—	17
Nepal	45	8	12
Netherlands	100	—	—
New Zealand	99	—	—
Nicaragua	31	13	18
Niger	16	9	8
Nigeria	40	24	25
Norway	100	—	—
Pakistan	21	28	12
Panama	46	9	23
Paraguay	49	5	17
Peru	43	17	26
Philippines	34	−9	27
Poland	87	—	4
Portugal	92	—	8
Romania	58	9	33
Russian Federation	76	—	9
Rwanda	50	11	19
Saudi Arabia	72	22	12
Senegal	42	8	13
Serbia	71	—	12
Sierra Leone	20	9	11
Singapore	98	—	—
Slovak Republic	84	—	10
Slovenia	98	—	—
South Africa	69	—	11
South Sudan	9	8	8
Spain	94	4	—
Sri Lanka	74	—	5
Sweden	100	—	—
Switzerland	98	—	—
Taiwan, China	94	—	5

Economy	Account ownership, 2017		
	Adults with an account (%)	Gap between men and women (percentage points)[a]	Gap between richer and poorer (percentage points)[b]
Tajikistan	47	10	14
Tanzania	47	9	16
Thailand	82	4	7
Togo	45	15	18
Trinidad and Tobago	81	15	6
Tunisia	37	17	26
Turkey	69	29	20
Turkmenistan	41	10	—
Uganda	59	13	20
Ukraine	63	4	16
United Arab Emirates	88	16	9
United Kingdom	96	—	—
United States	93	—	13
Uruguay	64	7	25
Uzbekistan	37	—	12
Venezuela, RB	73	7	22
Vietnam	31	—	18
West Bank and Gaza	25	19	22
Zambia	46	11	24
Zimbabwe	55	8	19

Source: Global Findex database.
Note: Only statistically significant gaps are shown. Gaps that fall within the reported margin of error for the survey in an economy are considered to be statistically insignificant (indicated by the use of a dash). For the margin of error for each economy, see table A.1 in the survey methodology section; see also note c in that table. Data for all indicators are available at http://www.worldbank.org/globalfindex.
a. A negative value indicates that a larger share of women than men have an account.
b. Gap in account ownership between adults in the richest 60 percent of households and those in the poorest 40 percent. Data are based on household income quintiles.

GLOBAL FINDEX GLOSSARY

able to raise emergency funds (%): Refers to the percentage of respondents who reported that in case of an emergency it is possible for them to come up with 1/20 of gross national income (GNI) per capita in local currency within the next month.

account (%): Refers to the percentage of respondents who reported having an account (by themselves or together with someone else) at a bank or another type of financial institution (see definition for *financial institution account*) or reported personally using a mobile money service in the past 12 months (see definition for *mobile money account*).

borrowed any money in the past year (%): Refers to the percentage of respondents who reported borrowing any money (by themselves or together with someone else) for any reason and from any source in the past 12 months.

borrowed formally (%): Refers to the percentage of respondents who reported borrowing any money from a bank or another type of financial institution, or using a credit card, in the past 12 months.

borrowed from family or friends (%): Refers to the percentage of respondents who reported borrowing any money from family, relatives, or friends in the past 12 months.

borrowed semiformally (%): Refers to the percentage of respondents who reported borrowing any money from a savings club in the past 12 months.

financial institution account (%): Refers to the percentage of respondents who reported having an account (by themselves or together with someone else) at a bank or another type of financial institution.[1]

has a credit card (%): Refers to the percentage of respondents who reported having a credit card.

has a debit card (%): Refers to the percentage of respondents who reported having a debit card.

has a national identity card (%): Refers to the percentage of respondents who reported having a national identity card. (To see the full list of IDs included in the survey by country, visit the Global Findex web page at http://www.worldbank.org/globalfindex.)

made or received digital payments in the past year (%): Refers to the percentage of respondents who reported using mobile money, a debit or credit card, or a mobile phone to make a payment from an account, or reported using the internet to pay bills or to buy something online, in the past 12 months. It also includes respondents who reported paying bills, sending or receiving remittances, receiving payments for agricultural products, receiving government transfers, receiving wages, or receiving a public sector pension directly from or into a financial institution account or through a mobile money account in the past 12 months.

mobile money account (%): Refers to the percentage of respondents who reported personally using a mobile money service in the past 12 months.[2]

no deposit and no withdrawal from an account in the past year (%): Refers to the percentage of respondents who reported neither a deposit into nor a withdrawal from their account in the past 12 months.

outstanding housing loan (%): Refers to the percentage of respondents who reported having an outstanding loan (by themselves or together with someone else) from a bank or another type of financial institution to purchase a home, an apartment, or land.

paid utility bills from an account (%): Refers to the percentage of respondents who reported personally making regular payments for water, electricity, or trash collection in the past 12 months directly from a financial institution account or using a mobile money account.

paid utility bills in cash only (%): Refers to the percentage of respondents who reported personally making regular payments for water, electricity, or trash collection in the past 12 months in cash only.

paid utility bills in the past year (%): Refers to the percentage of respondents who reported personally making regular payments for water, electricity, or trash collection in the past 12 months.

received a public sector pension in cash only (%): Refers to the percentage of respondents who reported personally receiving a pension from the government, military, or public sector in the past 12 months in cash only.

received a public sector pension in the past year (%): Refers to the percentage of respondents who reported personally receiving a pension from the government, military, or public sector in the past 12 months.

received a public sector pension into an account (%): Refers to the percentage of respondents who reported personally receiving a pension from the government, military, or public sector in the past 12 months directly into a financial institution account, into a card, or into a mobile money account.

received domestic remittances in the past year (%): Refers to the percentage of respondents who reported personally receiving any money in the past 12 months from a relative or friend living in a different area of their country. This includes any money received in person.

received government payments in cash only (%): Refers to the percentage of respondents who reported personally receiving payments from the government in the past 12 months in cash only.

received government payments in the past year (%): Refers to the percentage of respondents who reported personally receiving any payment from the government in the past 12 months. This includes payments for educational or medical expenses, unemployment benefits, subsidy payments, or any kind of social benefits (see definition for *received government transfers in the past year*). It also includes pension payments from the government, military, or public sector (see definition for *received a public sector pension in the past year*) as well as wages from employment in the government, military, or public sector (see definition for *received public sector wages in the past year*).

received government payments into an account (%): Refers to the percentage of respondents who reported personally receiving payments from the government in the past 12 months directly into a financial institution account, into a card, or into a mobile money account.

received government transfers in cash only (%): Refers to the percentage of respondents who reported personally receiving any financial support from the government in the past 12 months in cash only.

received government transfers in the past year (%): Refers to the percentage of respondents who reported personally receiving any financial support from the government in the past 12 months. This includes payments for educational or medical expenses, unemployment benefits, subsidy payments, or any kind of social benefits. It does not include a pension from the government, military, or public sector; wages; or any other payments related to work.

received government transfers into an account (%): Refers to the percentage of respondents who reported personally receiving any financial support from the government in the past 12 months directly into a financial institution account, into a card, or into a mobile money account.

received payments for agricultural products in cash only (%): Refers to the percentage of respondents who reported personally receiving money from any source for the sale of agricultural products, crops, produce, or livestock in the past 12 months in cash only.

received payments for agricultural products in the past year (%): Refers to the percentage of respondents who reported personally receiving money from any source for the sale of agricultural products, crops, produce, or livestock in the past 12 months.

received payments for agricultural products into an account (%): Refers to the percentage of respondents who reported personally receiving money from any source for the sale of agricultural products, crops, produce, or livestock in the past 12 months directly into a financial institution account, into a card, or into a mobile money account.

received payments from self-employment in cash only (%): Refers to the percentage of respondents who reported personally receiving money from their business, from selling goods, or from providing services (including part-time work) in the past 12 months in cash only.

received payments from self-employment in the past year (%): Refers to the percentage of respondents who reported personally receiving money from their business, from selling goods, or from providing services (including part-time work) in the past 12 months.

received payments from self-employment into an account (%): Refers to the percentage of respondents who reported personally receiving money from their business, from selling goods, or from providing services (including part-time work) in the past 12 months directly into a financial institution account, into a card, or into a mobile money account.

received private sector wages in cash only (%): Refers to the percentage of respondents who reported being employed in the private sector and receiving any money from an employer in the past 12 months in the form of a salary or wages for doing work in cash only.

received private sector wages in the past year (%): Refers to the percentage of respondents who reported being employed in the private sector and receiving any money from an employer in the past 12 months in the form of a salary or wages for doing work.

received private sector wages into an account (%): Refers to the percentage of respondents who reported being employed in the private sector and receiving any money from an employer in the past 12 months in the form of a salary or wages for doing work directly into a financial institution account, into a card, or into a mobile money account.

received public sector wages in the past year (%): Refers to the percentage of respondents who reported being employed by the government, military, or public sector and receiving any money from an employer in the past 12 months in the form of a salary or wages for doing work.

received wages in cash only (%): Refers to the percentage of respondents who reported receiving any money from an employer in the past 12 months in the form of a salary or wages for doing work in cash only.

received wages in the past year (%): Refers to the percentage of respondents who reported receiving any money from an employer in the past 12 months in the form of a salary or wages for doing work. This does not include any money received directly from clients or customers.

received wages into an account (%): Refers to the percentage of respondents who reported receiving any money from an employer in the past 12 months in the form of a salary or wages for doing work directly into a financial institution account, into a card, or into a mobile money account.

saved any money in the past year (%): Refers to the percentage of respondents who reported personally saving or setting aside any money for any reason and using any mode of saving in the past 12 months.

saved for old age (%): Refers to the percentage of respondents who reported saving or setting aside any money in the past 12 months for old age.

saved formally (%): Refers to the percentage of respondents who reported saving or setting aside any money at a bank or another type of financial institution in the past 12 months.

saved semiformally (%): Refers to the percentage of respondents who reported saving or setting aside any money in the past 12 months by using a savings club or a person outside the family.

sent domestic remittances in the past year (%): Refers to the percentage of respondents who reported personally sending any of their money in the past 12 months to a relative or friend living in a different area of their country. This can be money they brought themselves or sent in some other way.

sent or received domestic remittances in cash only (%): Refers to the percentage of respondents who reported personally sending any of their money in the past 12 months to, or receiving any of it from, a relative or friend living in a different area of their country in person, or through someone they know, and in cash only.

sent or received domestic remittances in the past year (%): Refers to the percentage of respondents who reported personally sending any of their money in the past 12 months to, or receiving any of it from, a relative or friend living in a different area of their country.

sent or received domestic remittances using an over-the-counter (OTC) service (%): Refers to the percentage of respondents who reported personally sending any of their money in the past 12 months to, or receiving any of it from, a relative or friend living in a different area of their country over the counter in a branch of their financial institution, through a mobile banking agent, or through a money transfer service.

sent or received domestic remittances using an account (%): Refers to the percentage of respondents who reported personally sending any of their money in the past 12 months to, or receiving any of it from, a relative or friend living in a different area of their country using a financial institution account or a mobile money account.

used a credit card in the past year (%): Refers to the percentage of respondents who reported using their own credit card in the past 12 months.

used a debit card to make a purchase in the past year (%): Refers to the percentage of respondents who reported using their own debit card directly to make a purchase in the past 12 months.

used a mobile phone or the internet to access an account in the past year (%): Refers to the percentage of respondents who reported using a mobile phone or the internet to make a payment, to make a purchase, or to send or receive money through their financial institution account or through the use of a mobile money service in the past 12 months.

used the internet to pay bills or to buy something online in the past year (%): Refers to the percentage of respondents who reported using the internet to pay bills or buy something online in the past 12 months.

Notes

1. Data on adults with a financial institution account include respondents who reported having an account at a bank or at another type of financial institution, such as a credit union, a microfinance institution, a cooperative, or the post office (if applicable), or having a debit card in their own name. The data also include an additional 3.93 percent of respondents in 2017 who reported receiving wages, government transfers, a public sector pension (included in 2017 data), or payments for agricultural products into a financial institution account in the past 12 months; paying utility bills or school fees from a financial institution account in the past 12 months; or receiving wages or government transfers into a card in the past 12 months.
2. Data on adults with a mobile money account include respondents who reported personally using services included in the GSM Association's Mobile Money for the Unbanked (GSMA MMU) database to pay bills or to send or receive money in the past 12 months. The data also include an additional 0.60 percent of respondents in 2017 who reported receiving wages, government transfers, a public sector pension (included in 2017 data), or payments for agricultural products through a mobile phone in the past 12 months.